MW00678649

Hate Me Now, Love Me Later

Jason Brown

Strategic Book Publishing and Rights Co.

Copyright © 2019 Jason Brown. All rights reserved.

No part of this book may be reproduced or transmitted in any form
or by any means, graphic, electronic, or mechanical, including
photocopying, recording, taping, or by any information storage
retrieval system, without the permission, in writing, of the publisher.
For more information, send an email to support@sbpra.net,
Attention Subsidiary Rights Department.

Strategic Book Publishing and Rights Co., LLC
USA | Singapore
www.sbpra.net

For information about special discounts for bulk purchases, please
contact Strategic Book Publishing and Rights Co. Special Sales, at
bookorder@sbpra.net.

ISBN: 978-1-950860-07-4

Book Design: Suzanne Kelly

"I recruited at Jason's school and signed one of his student athletes a few years back and got to know him and his program well. Having been a former JC assistant and head coach, I was very familiar with the trials and tribulations associated with helping JC young men transition to the four year college level socially, athletically, and academically. Although our styles in accomplishing the end result were very different, there were also many similarities. I never questioned Jason's genuine care and commitment for the young men in his charge. Hopefully you will see this too after reading this book."

—*Willie Fritz*
Head Football Coach, Tulane University

"JB is one of the most tireless workers, recruiters, men builders that I've encountered in our profession. His straightforward approach and his consistent, relentless attack on each day is what sets him apart from the rest."

—*Coach David Beatty*
Former Head Coach, Kansas University

"One of the hardest working coaches I know. An even greater man, who always has his players best interest at heart."

—*Darian Hagan*
Running Backs Coach, University of Colorado

"One of the best recruiters and offensive minds I've come across."

—*Derek Mason*
Head Coach, Vanderbilt University

"Jason has an innate ability to turn struggling football programs into SUCCESSFUL ones because of his shrewdness, tireless work ethic, unique communication skills and keen instincts dealing with players and staff."

—*Tammie Romstad*
Athletic Director, Independence Community College

"Jason's love for kids and passion for the game illustrated in this book is real."

—*Dr. Elio Mendoza*
Former Principal, Long Beach Cabrillo High School

"All coaching is, is taking a player to where he can't take himself, and it's amazing how far you can go when someone believes in you, and Coach Brown did that for me."

—*Jonathan Banks*
Quarterback, Tulane University

"Coach Brown has made a big impact on my life, which has prepared me for the next level and also has prepared me for life."

—*Emmit Gooden*
Defensive Tackle #93, University of Tennessee

"Without the discipline provided, most of us wouldn't of weathered the storm that we faced under Coach Jason Brown."

—*Alin Edouard*
Quarterback, University of Texas San Antonio (UTSA)

"Coach Brown is a real one. He did everything for me that he said he would and more. He is a genuine dude, and I think the world is too sensitive for him. I will always respect him for helping me get to where I am today."

—*Jermaine Johnson*
#1 JUCO player in America 2018-19 Class,
University of Georgia

"JB is a bit of an enigma. He'll berate young players in ways that border on cruel, but then turn around and work harder and more passionately to get those same players D1 scholarships."

—*Greg Whiteley*
Producer, Last Chance U

"One bad dude! Robust and uninhibited, what you see is what you get. Not the I-wish-I-would've/could've but the I-fricken-did-it guy. Totally authentic and you bet they ain't seen nothin' yet. It's going down!"

—*Don Pellum*
UCLA

Introduction

I guess my story began on the twenty-first day of February 1976, in Compton, California. I couldn't have asked for better parents: my mother, Cecilia Sims, and father, William Brown Jr. I was blessed growing up, even though, like anyone else, life was hard, especially having been raised in Compton during the precipice of the dope game in Los Angeles and the rise in gang violence. However, as I look back at my life, I would have it no other way! It toughened my skin and made me the person I am today; it's allowed me to use my upbringing and life experiences to help others.

I am going to share the highs and lows of my upbringing, my purpose on this planet, my rise, my demise, my only-to-rise-again attitude, along with the many trials and tribulations that come along with it. I do believe I was put on this great earth to

serve a purpose, like we all were. As for me, I believe I am a vessel to be used to share my experiences, tough-love approach, and real-world expectations with our youths, particularly those in the inner cities in our fine country.

I live how I coach, and that is abiding by this simple principle: WIN—What's Important Now!

I teach anyone I cross paths with how to WIN daily. We WIN in the community in which we live. We WIN in whatever it is we do for a living, and we WIN in our teachings daily with the youths.

When coaching, I preach WIN in the classroom first and foremost, WIN in our community, and WIN in the weight room, along with winning on the practice field.

If we WIN at the above-mentioned factors, then winning is easy on game days. Just as we WIN at the above-mentioned factors at our workplace, we can make it easy to WIN on weekends with our respective families.

Being a vessel for our youths is a very taxing position in life, and I have not only accepted it, I've attacked it head-on, as I do with all things life brings my way. I've accepted the challenge, yet I've also failed at it. I have been successful, but I will always be able to sleep at night knowing I put my best foot forward and helped at least one person along the way! As a young person/coach, I thought I could save and help everyone. That is just not the case, nor is it feasible. I used to tell my coaching staffs, "Don't try to save them all. You are spreading yourself too thin, and you will only be disappointed at day's end." That statement has been true over and over throughout my life, and I continue to use that approach in my life.

I hope you find my story of uphill battles, trials and tribulations, along with some good old blood, sweat, and tears very entertaining, but more importantly, very useful and informative.

Now, let's dive over the goal line and score a winner!

History Lesson

When I took my first head coaching position at the collegiate level, it was at my alma mater, Compton College. I was hired by two great men: Albert "Lefty" Olguin (the athletic director) and Lalo Mendoza (dean), who had coached and were very successful, to say the least. We all knew the challenges that the job presented. I was all in—excited, eager, cocky, arrogant, and egotistical—but my biggest flaw at that time was my youth, now that I look back at it. I thought I was bigger than the world, and Compton was my town, my school, and my people!

My dad went to Compton High School and Compton College with the likes of some very influential people, such as former NFL commissioner Pete Rozelle, Duke Snider (Dodger great), and Hugh McElhenny (NFL great). Athletes and commissioners weren't the only types of people raised in Compton during that time. Famous actors such as Marilyn Monroe, Kevin Costner, and James Coburn, just to name a few, also came from there. The younger generation had some famous actors and entertainers to look up to. Anthony Anderson, Todd Bridges, and comedian Paul Rodriguez, along with famous rappers like Dr. Dre, Eazy-E, The Game, Kendrick Lamar, and DJ Quik are just a few to have grown up in Compton—and don't forget two great tennis players, Venus and Serena Williams.

Compton has an enormous amount of history, and back when my father played high school football, the rules were a bit different. Not only were the rules on the field different, but the rules in the streets were different as well. In 1955, Compton High School played for the California Interscholastic Federation (CIF) championship in football vs. Compton Centennial High School. My father caught the only touchdown for Compton, but the game finished in a 6-6 tie. However, in 1955, the winner was determined by the team that had the most first downs. Compton Centennial had seven, while Compton finished with six, so Centennial was deemed the champs. Nowadays, we have what we call a California tiebreaker, and it's quite different than it was back then. The demographics were also very different. Compton High School had one black player, while Compton Centennial was an entirely black team at that time. Ten years later, in August of 1965, the Watts riots ravished Los Angeles, and it was at that time that Compton and Watts became commonly used together in neighborhood discussions throughout Los Angeles. Furthermore, the demographics began to change. Compton was a predominantly white neighborhood and a cattle town. It wasn't uncommon to see horses and buggies, along with cow pastures, within Compton neighborhoods at that time, but after the riots, more black people found Compton to be home. When I was born in 1976, Compton was predominantly black, and by the time I was able to run the streets in the mid-eighties, it was often called the murder capital of the United States.

We had a citywide curfew, and you weren't allowed to cross over Alondra Boulevard if you were from a Blood neighborhood and couldn't cross over Rosecrans Avenue if you were from a Crips neighborhood. Only folks from Compton will probably understand that statement, but it is what it is.

CHAPTER 1

Blood, Sweat, and Tears

Ibelieve in hard work, dedication, and determination. Having said that, I feel you need to approach everything you do with these principles in mind. I used these principles as a football coach and in life. I have broken down each job differently, but with the same ideology and mindset, and that mindset is to do what others say you cannot do!

I love taking over programs that have been down in the dumps, down on their luck, those that everyone tells you not to take, the programs that have upside—well, upside in my eyes, but that's all that matters at the end of the day. I love the challenge of taking over programs that nobody else would touch, creating cultures that are conducive to winning, and putting that place on the map! In my opinion, in order to come close to accomplishing any of the above-mentioned challenges, there must be a strong administrative staff, or a goal-oriented athletic director for you to work with, that has the same vision as you or is on the same respective page as you. Unfortunately, that wish list is not easy to find, but I can say that I have come across a few administrators like this, and, collectively, we've won in every program aspect imaginable.

Building football programs is like making business plans: you must have a dream, a vision, and a set of goals, but belief in yourself is most important. If you don't take the approach that you are in this for one sole reason, which is to help young people and all the good people that you cross paths with, then you are doing it for all the wrong reasons. I truly believe that. And just as you should when writing a business plan, it should have a vision and a mission statement that includes helping people and opening doors for whomever you encounter throughout the process, which includes assistant coaches, lower level/tier employees, as well as janitors, teachers, and any other subordinate coworkers.

I truly believe you must lead for others to follow, but lead by example, not with your tongue. You must prove to your team, coaches, and assistants that you are an all-in type of person, and cut your teeth as you would expect them to do. I lead with a democratic approach, not a dictatorship. Saying that, I do have non-negotiables, but we are in a results-oriented business, and the last time I checked, we either WIN the game or lose it, we either graduate our players or we don't, and we either earn our kids scholarships or we don't! Having said that, it is the same way in the business world. You either eat or get eaten—big fish eat little fish—so expectations should always remain high. Furthermore, your personal expectations must be higher than all others.

When building something from nothing, it requires blood, sweat, and tears, and it's much more rewarding when you build something into a winner by traveling this route, in my opinion. As I say that, I have reaped the benefits of the fruits of my labor, and I must say it feels good, but if you are expecting things to be handed to you without hiccups or trials and tribulations, then you are in the wrong business. We should always give our all, expect nothing less from our teams, and always put our best foot forward.

My first head college job was at Compton College, which as I mentioned was my alma mater as well. Compton has one of the winningest traditions of any junior college, and having won several Junior Rose Bowls, which was the biggest junior college bowl game back in the fifties and sixties, there was obviously a lot of tradition. However, I was inheriting a program that hadn't won a game in over two years. It was coming off probation and had been riddled with sanctions and allegations over the previous thirty years. So, my plate was always going to be full, which I fully accepted and looked forward to at that time.

My first order of business was to have a plan of attack, which I call a POA, and that POA was to organize myself, map out a three-year plan, and come up with an attack plan that was not only conducive to winning on the field, but to change the culture on the campus and in the community. Many other coaches would have probably turned left on Long Beach Boulevard, but I drove straight and made that right on Tartar Lane, which led to the campus of Compton College.

I was the only white player when I played in 1998 and 1999, and history repeated itself with me; I was the only white coach on the campus some ten years later. I took my pen and pad and did an evaluation of the facilities: the weight room, practice field, what equipment was needed, coaches' offices, what video hardware and software we had, and what we needed to be successful. I can say that we needed everything, and everything may have been an understatement!

I can tell you stories of when I played at Compton that many of you would never believe, but one story sticks out in my mind. We had a guy who played wide receiver. We were marching down the field in the second quarter, and I had just thrown this guy the ball. He ran out of bounds, handed the ball to the referee, and proceeded to take off his helmet and sprint toward the parking lot. Unbeknownst to us on the field, his car was being stolen in broad daylight from the parking lot literally thirty yards from the field.

Subsequently, an assistant coach ran after him, so we all thought it was going to be squashed and we would return to the game as planned, but this coach put this player in his car and took off after the stolen car. We continued the game, and about fifteen minutes later, we hear the crowd going crazy, and the coach is driving back into the parking lot, followed by our player. They had taken his car back from the car thief at the red light at the intersection of Santa Fe and Artesia Boulevard, before the thief could get on the 91 freeway. Our assistant coach and player got out of their car, opened the door, dragged the thief out, put a pretty good beating on him, and regained the vehicle. I always love telling that story over a few whisky and Cokes; it gets better and better.

Many stories can be told from my Compton tenure, from drinking forty-ounce beers in the locker room before games, to smoking weed on the busses as we traveled to and from road games. There was never a dull moment at Compton College! But it was for that reason alone that I am who I am, and I wouldn't have wanted it any other way.

The coaches' offices needed major reconstruction, so that would be my first order of business within my POA, even before I hired a full staff. So, I got to building with my own hands, and I hired one of my former players who did construction to put together some offices and a staff war room, along with a video room. It came out pretty nice, and I believe we got it done in one weekend.

I then began to interview a coaching staff, starting with my defensive coordinator, which was a no-brainer. I targeted a Compton legend, Keith Donerson, who at the time was the head coach at Compton Dominguez High School, the home of Richard Sherman, Tyson Chandler, The Game, Brandon Jennings, the Prince brothers, and many more great athletes. So, once I landed my DC, I went after my offensive line coach, and I hired a young man by the name of Mike Khoshkbariie, who assisted me at San Bernardino Valley College when I was the offensive coordinator the year prior. I then went after a veteran defensive backs coach by the name of Sean Fernandes, who actually coached me when I played at Compton College. I also went after an academic staff member who could mentor young inner-city student-athletes. I would go on to hire about ten coaches, and I believe we had the dynamic staff for what Compton needed at that time in 2008.

The blood and sweat continued, as we began to recruit with relentless effort throughout the spring and summer months. We brought in a great class, which included the likes of future NFL players Reggie Dunn, who played at Verbum Dei High School, and Super Bowl winner Akeem Ayers, who I also coached when I was the offensive coordinator at Verbum Dei some years before.

The next order of business was to order new equipment, and not only for practice. We needed new uniforms in a major way, so I hustled up a Nike deal and received new staff coaching gear, new player uniforms, and things that started to change the culture. It was much needed, but like anywhere that has been unsuccessful for a long period of time, it usually does need an overhaul. I love that portion of the job; it is only trumped by earning kids scholarships.

In year one at Compton College—not to spoil the end of this chapter, but it was actually my only year at Compton as head coach, and a year is actually an understatement; it was actually about nine months on the job, we will get to that in a bit—I continued to attack the position with full force. Hot on the recruiting trail we were "turning over rocks," as I like to say when referring to recruiting, which is what we did. We scrimmaged a good friend of mine by the name of Marguet Miller over at West Los Angeles Community College, and we rolled into that scrimmage with 186 players on the team, and when I say there wasn't a scrub on that roster, I truly mean it. We were loaded beyond belief regarding talent—one of my most talented rosters to date—but we had to instill a winning culture, because, at the end of the day, talent can only take you so far. Without discipline, the talent is negated by a more-disciplined program.

Well, the scrimmage was a good test for us, as Coach Miller runs a great program over at West LA, so we went on to prepare for a national power in Fullerton College, which was very talented and very disciplined, so we were going to have our hands full in game one of the 2008 season. We came out and moved the ball with great efficiency and had over six hundred yards total offense that game, but we came up short and lost 35-30. I immediately told the team that the difference in the scoreboard was strictly knowing how to WIN. Our program didn't know how to WIN yet, and it was apparent. Even though it was a new-and-improved Compton College team, we weren't quite ready to compete with the big dogs. I knew that but couldn't accept it, so I used every motivational tactic in the book, and I shortly figured out that the "book" didn't have what I needed. So, I quickly found out I was all that I would ever need, and motivating players, along with your staff, is a must as a head coach. If you cannot motivate personnel, you can't coach, and I live by that statement.

We had no schedule break, and for game two we hosted a loaded Pasadena City team, which actually won a bowl game that season. We couldn't be stopped on offense and exploded for a sixty-point effort and beat Pasadena something like 60-45, a true shootout, which also was played in 100-degree heat. It was an exhausting game, and I used all three timeouts in consecutive order with under one minute to play in the first half. It was a huge program-building victory, and, knowing who we played next on our schedule, we surely needed it.

ELCO, El Camino Community College, the number-one-ranked team in the country at that time, was who we had to play. This story is legendary. We had some big-time talent, as did they, but if you refer back to my POA and changing the culture, I stated that we got new uniforms from Nike. Well, that was only partially true, we had *home* uniforms, and our first two ballgames were at home, so we hadn't yet received our away uniforms, so this would turn into a true shitshow. The El Camino game would be a very eventful week, to say the least.

It started on the Sunday after we beat Pasadena City. The traditional way to trade film back in 2008 was to meet halfway between the two schools and trade VHS cassette tapes, so that is what we did. I remember it like it was yesterday. I had a few friends on the staff over at ELCO, so we agreed to meet up and trade the film. Everything went fine. We both went back to our respective schools and started to break down the film and prepare scouting reports. That Sunday would be one of the longest Sundays of my life. My friend over at ELCO called me later on that evening and proceeded to tell me that his head coach, a man named John Featherstone, wasn't happy with our film. As a head coach, I always have taken amazing pride in presenting our programs with dignity, pride, professionalism, and being as courteous as possible with other schools, but this was a case of absolute disrespect and had me in a very foul mood, to say the least. I continued to field phone calls from ELCO's coaching staff. Finally, I got Coach Featherstone on the phone, and we proceeded to curse each other out, and at that point I told him I would return the film and we would see their asses Saturday.

Earlier that year, Compton College had lost its accreditation academically, so Governor Schwarzenegger awarded ELCO the school's rights academically. So, what does that mean, you ask? It means all the academic programs were under EL Camino's watch, and that went for the classes my players took, to the graduation process and policy. Along with that, the Compton College campus police were now El Camino police, which rubbed many people in the community the wrong way. Well, by ELCO now having control of Compton College, it was very hard to recruit against them, but we had whipped their ass in recruiting that year, and I turned over rocks like I had never done to that point, but it wasn't enough when playing an established powerhouse program such as ELCO. We needed extra motivation but would again get bombarded with bad news on the Friday's walk-through prior to Saturday's game. I received a call from my AD, and he informed me that our away Nike uniforms hadn't come in yet. So, I asked why,

and where were they? He told me he didn't know. After dig-
ging around and doing some research, Nike informed us that
the uniforms had been delivered four days prior. We called
people, we went searching on campus, and yet nothing! Come
to find out, the uniforms had been delivered to our main campus, which ironically was now El Camino Community College, so not only was there beef regarding traded film, now
they purposely held our away uniforms so we couldn't use
them in the upcoming game.

So, what was I to do? By rule, we had to submit our roster jersey numbers each week. I didn't have the correct jersey
numbers to match the practice set of uniforms that we had in
the equipment room, so I had to take the entire day to resubmit
new jersey numbers, so the player who usually wore number 1
was now 86, and so on and so forth. You can imagine the mood
this put me in. So, I wanted to be the bigger man and call Coach
Featherstone himself, and since ELCO was blue and silver, we
had no conflicting colors, so I asked to wear our home maroon
uniforms. He said, "Hell no!" and hung up. I just laughed and
knew I had to come up with some type of crazy motivational
speech to get my guys to beat their asses.

In life, there will always be trials and tribulations, and I have a saying: "When it rains, it pours." Saturday afternoon it would truly pour rain on our parade. We arrived for team meal, team walk-through, and normal game-day prep, but this game day would have a wrench thrown our way, as if we needed it. As we waited for our busses to arrive to take us over to ELCO, my mind was blown away by what I actually saw pulling onto our campus to pick us up. Once the busses got closer, I said to my staff, "You gotta be shittin' me!" There were two 1972 Greyhound busses that had duct-taped seats and, of course, had no air-conditioning. Mind you, it's September in Los Angeles, so it's eighty-five degrees at 4:00 p.m. We still laugh about that evening to this day. So, as we left campus, we turned out of the facility and the defensive bus leaned onto one side. I thought it was literally tipping over. I thought, "What a day this is going to be!" Remember, ELCO was basically our CEO, and guess who ordered these busses that night? Yes, ELCO ordered them.

We kicked it off at 7:00 p.m., so we make it over to ELCO, which was just a twenty-minute drive from Compton, and I am greeted by ELCO's athletic director, who immediately requested our new roster numbers on paper. So, as you all can probably imagine, I lost my shit and literally cursed him out about as bad as a person could curse someone out. My piss was getting hot, and I knew whatever I was going to do to get my team amped up was going to have to be off the top of my head, and I have come to find out that the more genuine it is, the more realistic it is conveyed to your team.

I pulled my equipment manager to the side and asked him to set aside a jersey, a set of pads, and a helmet for me. He asked why. I just said, "Don't worry about it. Do it, please." So I addressed the team after we warmed up. I got the team on a knee and let them know how I felt regarding the jerseys and the bus, how we are being called ELCO's JV team, due to the accreditation situation, and I go on a rant about how we are being fucked and "Y'all better WIN this for me," and so on and so forth. My kids literally went bananas and were jumping into lockers, etc., but what I did next is what allowed our team to have a fighting chance that eventful night.

I yelled over at the equipment manager to throw me that bag he had put away for me. Inside that bag was obviously the helmet, pads, and jersey, so I put that shit on and told them I was leading them out through the tunnel, and they lost their fucking minds! As I proceeded to lead us out, the cheerleaders were holding the banner that we broke as a tradition each game. Well, guess who broke the banner first this game? Me! I did! As I broke the banner in coaching slacks, pads, a game jersey, and helmet, the first person I saw when I hit the sideline with my team was none other than Pete Carroll, the USC head coach, and his wife, who were there to watch us play. He said, "Jesus, JB, is that you?" I could only laugh and hope this was enough to pull off a monster upset.

We deferred, as I usually do with coin tosses, and they took the football first. I told my DC that they were going to run a play pass and to go cover zero and bring the house, and that's exactly what we did! We had an outside linebacker from South Carolina hit their QB so hard that he was legitimately knocked out in the air as the ball squirted out into the arms of our defensive lineman, who proceeded to score a defensive TD to start the game. Remember when I said my downfall as a young head coach was indeed my youth? Well, that is about as honest as I can be. After we scored, the referee blew a whistle that overturned the TD, and after conversing amongst the crew, they said the QB's arm was going forward, so second down it would be. But as all this was happening, I was literally at the fifty-yard line, halfway out on the field yelling obscenities at Coach Featherstone and letting him know his "JV" team was here as promised!

We went on to have a good old-fashioned shootout that evening, and, just as we did vs. Fullerton in game one, we came up short once again. We lost 37-35. My team just wasn't quite ready to beat the big dogs on the road that night, but everyone was put on notice that night that JB was a great recruiter, a great play caller, and a great motivator!

Tears

At 1-2 on the season, I went about my business as usual, prepping for San Diego Southwestern College, which was our next opponent. In life, as previously stated, we will have trials and tribulations, and my life was about to have one of those situations once again. My AD, Lefty, called me into the office as he routinely would. I just walked into his office with a facial expression of a coach who just lost to ELCO two days prior, but I would quickly find out that this was no routine visit. Lefty was with ELCO administrators and Human Resources to let me know that I had been fired as the head football coach at Compton College for lying on my application some ten months prior. I was dumbfounded, so obviously I was pissed off and confused. I said I never lied on any application. Well, they proceeded to tell me that I had a felony charge on my

application, and that I didn't check the box that stated such. I said that I never had any felony, that I was accused of some crimes years ago, but I had beat that case in a jury trial, and at the time of the application, I had a felony pending, so this was a witch hunt. I was about as sad as I've ever been in life, and Lefty wasn't much happier. I will tell the story of the accusations later.

So, I would pack my office up and turn in my keys as the head coach of the Tartars of Compton College and go figure out my next move. If it were only that easy! I had recruited basically 120 players myself and had made deals with parents and promised players that I would graduate them and get them scholarships. So, being a man of my word is what I was going to be, regardless if I was the coach or not. I set up a private meeting with the team right on Artesia Boulevard, through the fence that led to the football practice field. As I stood there in street clothes, I apologized to the team and staff alike. There were many tears shed that afternoon, and I quickly realized this coaching thing is what I was put on this earth to do! So, coaching it would be! I quickly knew that JUCO football was what I wanted to do forever, because the impact you have on young people is greater than any other venue, and I knew I was a vessel to help kids achieve their goals.

I know you are reading this and probably saying, "He was just fired." Well, indeed I was fired, but it was a wake-up call, and I knew that I needed this platform to help young people achieve their goals in life. So, I would fight like hell to get back in the head-coaching seat once again.

CHAPTER 2

Do What You Want to Do, Not What You Have to Do

Father William Brown and mother Cecilia Sims at Fort Hays State.

My father always told me to "Do what you want to do, not what you have to do." He was referring to a trade, a profession, or means of employment. I truly believe this statement and live by it. I have always sacrificed for the greater good, and the pursuit of my "want to" and coaching is no different. You will face some hard times, question yourself at times, and ask yourself if this is even worth it. I asked myself this very thing many times, but I stuck it out, and it paid off. It especially pays off when you see young people get rewarded with scholarships and earn degrees after the hard work, determination, and dedication.

I finished playing football professionally with the Bakersfield Blitz of the Arena Football League, and after playing in its inaugural season and winning the conference, I had to do some soul-searching and figure out what it was I truly wanted to do in life. I went back to school during the off-season before giving my head coach, who happened to be long-time NFL cornerback James Fuller, an answer regarding my future. I felt this was best at the time, since I only needed a semester's worth of classes to complete my bachelor's degree in physical education. I completed my degree and realized I hadn't worked out, thrown a football, or lifted a weight in months, and football as a player was no longer important to me—or perhaps I just lost the love of playing the sport.

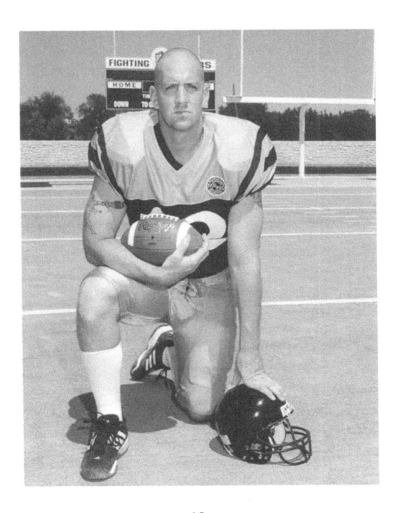

After having a few cups of coffee in NFL camps and NFL Europe, arena leagues, and traveling the country and abroad, I realized football had been great to me, allowed me to earn a degree, and allowed me to see the countryside and Europe, along with the beautiful island of Hawaii twice. I just thought, "Maybe my calling is helping guys like me reach their potential in life, either on or off a football field." So, I made a decision to get into coaching, and this coaching business is colder than the dope game, if you ask me. It's a "who you know, not what you know" business. It's about sacrifices and self-glory, because 90 percent of the work that you do goes unappreciated and unnoticed, and at the end of the day, you are either the goat or the hero. Coaching jobs are usually offered at the most peculiar times. They can be in a grocery store, at a clinic, or working a camp, but my first coaching job was offered to me at a strip club, believe it or not. I'm leaving names out of this one, but I accepted!

My first job was at my high school alma mater Artesia High School in Lakewood, California. I lived most of my teenage years in Lakewood with my father and, prior to that, with my mother and father when they were married in a nice house in Lakewood, which was attached to the elementary school that I attended, which was called Willows Elementary. Artesia High School was the same school that my older brother attended some ten years prior, and now was a completely different demographic. Artesia bordered a rough Hispanic neighborhood called Hawaiian Gardens. There were ongoing race riots at school and in the streets between the high school and Hawaiian Gardens. We were always on edge as kids; we just wanted to play sports, go to school, and try and earn a scholarship.

As previously mentioned, my father was raised in Compton and went to school there. On the other hand, my mother grew up in Bell Gardens, another inner-city suburb within Los Angeles County. My father and I lived in quite a few different places. We would go back and forth between Compton, Lakewood, and Huntington Beach. After the divorce, my mother went her own way and hit the dating circuit, and my father did the same. They were cordial toward one another after the divorce but not that fond of each other. I think deep down inside, each still loved the other, because, at the end of the day, I don't think you can just ignore your feelings.

I believe I was about eleven years old when my mother and father went through their divorce and went on their respective ways. I chose to live with my father and moved to Huntington Beach with him, but only for about six months. We both hated living there for various reasons. For one, we thought the people were stuck up and a bit too high class for us, so we figured out very quickly that this city wasn't for us. We moved back to Lakewood and rented a condo while I finished high school at Artesia.

My mother was living in a nice part of Long Beach in a community called Marina Pacifica. It was upscale and on the waterfront. I frequently visited, but wasn't too fond of her boyfriend, so that didn't last too long. Although my mother had introduced me to some of the nicer things in life, I was a bit in over my head there. I didn't think I belonged at some of the prestigious places she took me.

My mother's boyfriend at the time was a well-known businessman in Long Beach, and he had connections all over, from private country clubs, to big time restaurants—one was the well-known Italian spot called Trani's in San Pedro, California. Trani's is owned and operated by Phil Trani, a great, great man. I still talk to Phil to this day, and when I was the head coach at Long Beach Cabrillo, he fed my entire team on road games. He fed us his famous pasta and garlic bread, along with his world-famous calamari, which he knows I love. Phil is a very well-loved and well-known sports fanatic, and his restaurant is widely known as a big time USC and UCLA hangout. My mother took me to these types of places and introduced me to guys such as Tommy Lasorda, Jamaal Wilkes, John Wooden, and many more.

I get many of my traits from my mother. She doesn't take any shit from anyone and is as feisty as it gets. I often heard her screaming obscenities from the crowd as I played on the field,

so you can imagine how loud she was. She was always supportive and loved me unconditionally but ran a tight ship at the
house as I was growing up. She will argue with me that this next
story didn't happen, but I know it did, so here goes.

I often got up late at night to have a glass of water. She hated
that I left the empty glass on the kitchen counter, so she would
come grab my ass by the ear and drag me to the kitchen to wash
it and put it away! To her credit, she was working two jobs as a
nurse, and the hours of a nurse are very erratic and lengthy, so
I give her a pass.

After I graduated and found out that I was going to have to
attend a JUCO, we moved and rented a home on the other side
of Lakewood, near our rival high school: Lakewood High. We
always looked at this side of town as stuck up, upper class, and
people who thought they were too good for our side of town, but
the house was nice, and my father liked it.

My first job was a head-coaching job: leading the freshman
football team at Artesia. I was fresh off a playing career and
thought my shit didn't stink whatsoever. I thought I could walk
on water and not get wet! I quickly hired some of my close
friends to assist me, and we hit the ground running. I knew what
I knew, so I told myself to run this program like programs that
I had familiarity with and instill program values from coaches I
learned from along the way.

We began to instill discipline, conditioning regimens, and a
weightlifting plan of attack. We had about nineteen kids on the
team, but some feisty, quality kids, and a few ringers within the
group. We had a savvy QB, a few really good athletes, and some
good RBs. So, now I started to evaluate our offensive and defensive lines. We were small and weak, so I said, "Screw it. Let's
go spread offensively, play everything in front of us on defense,
get the kids to play hard, and see what happens."

One of Compton's rap legends, Eazy-E, had a few sons who
lived in Lakewood. Ironically enough, we had a player on this
team by the name of Eric Wright, which was also Eazy-E's real
name, and we quickly found out it was indeed Eazy-E's son. Eric
Wright was a tough, hardnosed player for me. He had great vision

and soft hands. He was one of the immediate leaders on our team and had a great freshman campaign for us. We also had a plethora of good athletes, and I thought we would be pretty good.

The freshmen at Artesia had been bad for years. Artesia was known for being a national powerhouse in basketball. Players such as Ed O'Bannon, Charles O'Bannon, Avondre Jones, Jason Kapono, and James Harden played there, so you can understand if football, especially freshman football, wasn't high on the expectation list. But that didn't sit well with me. Moral victories didn't sit well with me, so I was like, "Screw this! Let's go WIN, and just maybe we can create some good football players along the way."

We had a good season, going 6-4 in the Suburban League, with the likes of freshman powerhouses such as La Mirada, Mayfair, and Bellflower High Schools. We took La Mirada, which went undefeated, to the brink of defeat, losing it in the last seconds, even though La Mirada used a running clock on every other opponent that season, meaning they were beating every team so badly that they just ran the clock continuously. Taking them to the wire showed me that these kids bought in, believed in what we did, and played hard for me, so I was very pleased with a group of just nineteen kids.

The varsity staff quickly recognized that I had an eye for talent and that I frankly knew more football than they did, so they would come pick my brain offensively and ask me to come and coach with them. I declined, but I did take a particular player under my wing during this time by the name of Orlando Scandrick, who has had a pretty good NFL career with the Dallas Cowboys, Washington Redskins, and KC Chiefs. Orlando knew the varsity program wasn't very good, and his mother was going to shop him to other high schools, so I helped him and his mother pick a school. I took him to Dominguez High School and Lynwood High School, but his mother wasn't having it, so they chose to go to Los Alamitos High School, and the rest is history. Orlando's choice paid dividends for him and his family. Orlando would go on and play at Boise State University, where he was named a Freshman All-American for his efforts.

Jason Brown

My first job was short-lived. I was ready to challenge myself. So after saying my goodbyes, I quickly called one of my mentors in life: Cornell Ward. Coach Ward, who was my head coach at Compton College, is a man who is dear to me and taught me a lot about life—and, oh yeah, was a pretty damn good coach as well. I learned the recruiting game from this man. This man could go get him some talent; that is what he was known for—well, known for—regarding football, but Coach Ward was also very known throughout the streets of Los Angeles for much, much more than just football. Coach Ward and a man you may know as "Freeway" Rick Ross were best friends, and let's just say that I was basically taught the streets, and how to survive and hustle, by these men many years prior to my coaching days.

Coach Ward was still the head coach at Compton College, and I felt I was ready to coach college football, so he invited me up to his office. We talked and felt that my best option

Coach Cornell Ward and Freeway Rick Ross at Indy.

was to go be a varsity high school offensive coordinator first. We had a good friend who just took the head job at Verbum Dei High, a perennial powerhouse in basketball and football throughout the seventies, eighties, and even the nineties. Verb was known for great talent, such as Hardy Nickerson, Andre Miller, Roy Hamilton, Kenechi Udeze, Vernon Maxwell (former NFL Rookie of Year), and a guy who may have been one of the biggest street legends known to man by the name of Raymond Lewis. These men were all coached by a legend named Lalo Mendoza, who later in life hired me at Compton College, and who comes from a football family. Lalo's younger brothers also coached with him at Verb during this time, and later in life they too became head coaches. Lalo's younger brother, Kiki Mendoza, became the head coach at local powerhouse St. John Bosco High School, and Elio Mendoza would later become my boss at Long Beach Cabrillo High School, but that story is yet to come.

So, Verbum Dei High School it was. I quickly installed my offense in a rather uniquely structured program—meaning, at Verbum Dei, they had a mandatory work-study program for all students. So, one day per week a different class would travel to a different location and work an eight-hour shift as you would as an adult. I thought it was a good skill to have and learn, but it was not easy to work with as a football coach. We had a time disadvantage, but I was happy for the kids who gained powerful real-life, hands-on experiences. So, we practiced later in the day, which meant lifting weights and practicing back to back, which was daunting on our kids, especially a group comprised of mostly sophomores, a few juniors, with, I believe, one senior. The sophomores, however, were guys like Super Bowl winning linebacker and former UCLA star Akeem Ayers, who I was very close with during my year at Verbum Dei. He also had a younger brother, Kevin, who would play JUCO, then go to Arizona State, and later play in the CFL. Akeem played tight end for me on offense and defensive end on defense. I believe he had like twenty TDs on offense as a sophomore, and thirty-five sacks on defense, which at the time was a CIF record.

The first time I saw him doing cone drills, I told one of my buddies, "This kid will play in the NFL."

My buddy said, "Yeah, right."

I said, "Okay, watch!"

Akeem played for many years in the NFL and won a Super Bowl with the New England Patriots.

I was also fortunate enough to have coached kids such as Reggie Dunn, who also played in the NFL and played in JUCO at Compton College for me. Reggie would go on to break NCAA records as a kick returner at the University of Utah. Reggie was blazing fast, with great ball skills, and all he needed was the weight room and toughness at that young age. Our QB was a kid named Curtis, who was a Carson kid, had a strong arm, and could run, but was a QB coach's nightmare. He was a lefty! A lefty QB is never easy to coach, or desired, but Curtis was a great young kid with a tremendous upside. He had a very good sophomore season for us. I had tough-minded leaders as well, including a kid by the name of Marquis Bradley. He was a hard-nosed physical kid who played just about every position on the field for us and helped us WIN the league as a bunch of sophomores.

We would eventually meet our maker when we faced Oaks Christian High School in the second round of the CIF playoffs, led by the high-school-great QB Jimmy Clausen and linebacker Clay Mathews Jr, and coached by the likes of Clay Mathews Sr. The talent on that team was unbelievable. This is the school that later housed Wayne Gretzky's kids, Will Smith's kids, and Joe Montana's kids, so we were facing a resourceful program on top of a very talent-rich football team. Oaks Christian dominated us in every facet and blew us out. It was a great experience for a group of young men, and Kendrick Knox, who was the head coach, managed that team with great leadership. I will always be thankful for Coach Knox for hiring me.

As I give you my coaching resume throughout this chapter, the untold story is how I was earning money to live on. This is where the true sacrifice came into play, where the "Do what I want to do, not what I have to do" came into play, because, at the end of the day, I would either have to quit coaching football and work forty hours a week at some warehouse job, or follow my heart and dreams. I would do odd jobs just to get by until the job I wanted came open. I never wanted to teach in a classroom setting, so I never got my teaching credential. So, although I have coached at high schools, I was never a teacher at a public high school due to not having my credential. I did, however, teach at a few private high schools, one being Sacred Heart in Lincoln Heights, a small suburb of Los Angeles. Sacred Heart was also an all-girls school, but that is an entirely different book in its own right!

I wanted to coach JUCO ball, and that is what I did. I left Verbum Dei after one season and took my talents to East Los Angeles Community College in East L.A. I was hired by a man named Marguet Miller (pronounced Mar-gay), and I would go on to learn a lot about coaching offense and recruiting, but the most important thing I learned from Coach Miller was how hard he worked on helping kids earn scholarships, and how much effort he put into helping kids. I loved that about him and took that trait from him as I grew as a coach. This was in 2005, and we worked for a man named Ruben Ale, who was a well-known Polynesian coach from our area. He had a brother named Arnold Ale, who played at UCLA and would go on to have a cup of tea in the NFL.

Ruben Ale was pretty much a dictator and rubbed many of the staff members the wrong way, so once that season ended, I took the offensive coordinator position at San Bernardino Valley College. This is where my firing at Compton College becomes relevant. The year is 2006. During the 2005 season at East Los Angeles, I lost my mentor, my best friend, my father, William Brown Jr., during spring ball. It was a very hard time for me, because he battled cancer for years, and as his stubborn ass fought it like no other had fought pancreatic cancer before, he would still drink daily and cuss like a sailor, but at the end of the day, he did what he wanted to, not what he had to do. My father would succumb to cancer and pass away in my arms on the morning of April 18, 2005.

Jason Brown

This day is a teachable moment for coaches and players alike. I was at practice later that day, a few hours after my father's passing, and took it head-on like the man I was when I accepted the position at East Los Angeles College. I could have taken a week off, or what have you, but my father wouldn't have allowed it, and it just isn't in my DNA to miss something, especially a coaching job that I wanted and accepted. My point is, when your players miss a practice, or meetings, or study-hall sessions, or whatever the fuck you require of them, you better ask them this question: "Do you really love football?" And if they answer yes, which they will do, you say, "No you don't, because you wouldn't of missed my fucking meeting, son!" Or that history class or your trainer's appointment! That is what I tell kids to this day, because if I could not miss practice the day of my father's passing, then your ass can wake up and get to weights, or follow directions and go to study hall, or do what's best for the program that you have chosen to be a part of. I tell kids every day that the real world is going to hit them in the mouth very soon, and if you show up to work late, or miss work, your ass is going to get fired, so don't start a bad habit now as a student-athlete.

In 2006, I accepted the position at San Bernardino Valley College, and this year would be the worst year of my life. It wasn't the football, coaching, or the people. I loved the kids I coached that year. I recruited some NFL talent to SBVC, but that year hit me hard. It wasn't too long after the passing of my father. I basically came from a poor family, to say the least. We didn't have much, but what we did have we appreciated. My father was a diesel mechanic, and my mother was a nurse who worked in the convalescent side of the medical field. So, fancy cars and big houses are something we never had, but we were okay with it. We had food, and we would take an occasional vacation to a lake or something, so I couldn't complain. My point is, when my father passed away, he didn't have a will, power of attorney, life insurance, or anything. So, in 2006, whatever materialistic items I possessed were from him, and basically I ended up having my truck repossessed, my credit cards cancelled, and was eventually evicted from my apartment in Long Beach.

My world had been turned upside down, and I had to figure out what I was to do. I could tuck my head and go work a nine-to-five job, or suck it up, quit feeling sorry for myself, and go attack life as I always did. I chose the latter and continued to pursue my "want to," thinking optimistically as I often did when I went to sleep each night. So, I took this position at San Bernardino Valley College, immediately started to turn over rocks on the recruiting trail, and went after a QB, of course. I had my eye on the two best QBs in the Inland Empire that year, who were Mike Stadler from Redland East Valley High School, and Brad Sorensen from Colton High School. These two had traveled completely different roads to get to where they wanted to be.

Mike lived with his mother in what was basically a trailer home in Redlands, and Brad lived with his entire family—brothers, mother, and father—in the Grand Terrace area of San Bernardino County. Brad grew up in a Mormon family and was raised with a few older brothers who were very talented players as well; one had an NFL shot with the Colts before suffering a career-ending injury, and the other actually played for us at SBVC and was Brad's TE target and actually named All-American that season. Brad had a younger brother who happens to be Daniel Sorensen, the starting safety for the KC Chiefs as I write this. Brad would go on to play at Southern Utah after he served his Mormon mission. Brad was later drafted by the San Diego Chargers and backed up David Rivers for several years before being picked up by the Vikings.

Colton High School had four future NFL players on that team: Brad Sorensen, Allen Bradford, Shareece Wright, and Jimmy Smith—a damn good high school football team, to say the least. Mike Stadler played for a good team himself. Redlands East Valley put kids in college every year, and always had a solid program, but Colton was the team to beat that year. It came down to a game between the two QBs I was recruiting. Brad was six five, surprisingly athletic for a tall, lanky white

Brad Sorensen, Mike Stadler, and Santos Gonzalez at San Bernardino Valley College in 2006.

kid, but had tremendous poise, great savvy, and was a natural leader with a big-time NFL arm. Mike was about six two, average athletically, and could throw the ball with good accuracy, but he wasn't on Brad's level regarding a natural skill set. You can't teach nuts and guts, and that's what Mike had. Mike led his team to do what was thought to be the impossible that season and beat Brad's Colton squad in a shootout.

I wanted both kids, along with a third quarterback I had coached back in Long Beach by the name of Santos Gonzalez, who was a true triple option QB with a cannon for an arm. I brought all three QBs in to compete that year, and they all did a hell of job for me. Brad was the clear-cut favorite to start, and start is what he did, breaking several SBVC records that season.

The second major recruit I needed to go after was a kid who was making quite the name for himself in the Inland Empire that season by the name of Erin Madden, probably the most complete running back I have ever seen or coached. Erin played at AB Miller for a buddy of mine, so I had an inside track and went in with guns blazing to land this phenom. Erin was a great kid, a street kid who came from nothing, who was raised by his mother who would work tirelessly to put food on the table for him. I really wanted to help this kid and prove my worth to him.

Well, the worst year of my life continued to get worse. The summer of 2006 approached, and we started summer football practice. Times were getting hard. Gas prices were at an all-time high, and I had to make ends meet, so I tried to sell a bunch of personal belongings online. I began trying to sell the ten thousand dollars' worth of stereo equipment and TVs that had been in my truck that got repossessed. It all seemed to be going fine, until I tried to cash a check that was sent to me for my stereo. I come to find out that this check was part of a huge payroll scam that went sour. To make a long story short, I was arrested and charged with eight counts of felony robbery, identity theft, and fraud. I was released on my own recognizance, and the fight of my life began.

I had no money, I had no income, and, besides a small coaching stipend, I had no other source of income. So, bills that were mine, plus credit card debt and a home loan that was in my father's name before he passed away, were all now on me to figure out. I got stuck with the debt, which is an entirely different story altogether. My credit was shot, my life was in shambles, and I had nobody to lean on besides my mother, who was just retiring at this time, and she had already done more than enough for me and my foolish ways. I was issued a pro-bono attorney to represent me during the fight of my life, and he was a wet-behind-the-ears, young, scared guy who was going up against the DA in Riverside County, which was no joke! I was thinking in my mind, "I am fucked!"

The season came and went; we finished 5-5. With the athletic department in shambles—there was the crooked AD, a politically incorrect dean of students, along with a head coach who was going through a midlife crisis on the home front—life couldn't have been much worse. When it rains, it pours, and it started to pour down on me once again. As I fought in court every week for my freedom and good name, I was accused of stealing the head coach's computer from his office, which was not only an impossibility, it was a slap in my face, to say the least. I was asked to take a lie detector test for the District of San Bernardino. I obliged and passed it with flying colors, so as soon as I passed that test, I obviously got back to campus as fast as humanly possible to curse out the head coach and the dean of students, which I happily did. I handed them my letter of resignation and took Erin Madden, Dustin Blount, and Jacoby Hammond with me to my new place of employment. I was headed home!

Compton College had made me their offensive coordinator, but it wasn't working for my mentor, Coach Ward. He had left a few years prior for Los Angeles Southwest College, so I was going to work for a man who coached me at Compton by the name of Angelo Jackson. Angelo was a good man and always looked out for me. He and his wife were good people and helped me get back on my feet. I will always appreciate Coach J. He had a hard job at Compton replacing Coach Ward. He didn't have the support Coach Ward had, and he had to deal with a lot of politics and a new dean of students and president. I just wanted to help him WIN and recruit kids Compton would normally not recruit. I brought some big-time talent into Compton, not only from the Los Angeles inner-city areas, but I went out of state and brought in some big-time talent from Florida, Georgia, Louisiana, and South Carolina.

We looked promising that 2007 season, but then Coach Jackson was hit with an academic report that deemed half our team ineligible. That was basically the demise of Coach Jackson, as he was fired. Compton had hired a new AD by the name of Albert "Lefty" Olguin, who to this day is one of the finest human beings on this green earth.

I grew up on the campus of Compton College, as my father and uncle both played at Compton College and had won Junior Rose Bowl games. The field at Compton College was named after my great-uncle Tay Brown. The teachers, administrators, and police department on campus were all my good friends. I grew up a Tartar, and there was nobody who knew the ins and outs like I did. I felt at home. It felt good to be home, and I wanted to do what my family accomplished, and that was to WIN a bowl game.

As my court case continued, I finally was appointed a jury trial, and we went to war. After a long, drawn-out case, the jury found me not guilty, and all charges were dropped. I filled out my employment application at Compton College in November of 2007, but apparently I filled it out untruthfully, which wasn't by design or on purpose. I beat the case in early December, and I was named head coach at Compton in mid-December; I was the youngest head coach in junior college. I already told the story of my POA and how I rebuilt Compton College, but now you know what led to me later being fired. Regardless, in January of 2008, we hit the recruiting trail hard, turned over the proverbial rocks, and landed a great recruiting class.

Erin Madden, who I had brought with me from San Bernardino Valley, was living in a home in Compton with several other players and, unfortunately, some non-players. The non-players were robbing houses in Torrance, and Erin ended up being a victim of circumstance. This Saturday morning, I cancelled workouts to give our team a rest—well, in the inner-city, that was a bad idea. Furthermore, it's a bad idea for junior college kids, because junior college kids can't afford any time off, or they do stupid shit such as this. Well, during this robbery attempt, Erin was told he was going to a girl's house. He stayed in the car while his friends were in the house. Unbeknownst to him, the police pull up with lights blaring and arrested Erin on the spot. The police had already staked out the house and were onto the kids who were performing these home burglary attempts.

While Erin was being booked for burglary at the police station in Torrance, his friends were running from the police through Torrance. When the Torrance PD finally caught up to the kids they were chasing, as you can imagine, it wouldn't end well. A 911 call from the burglary suspect stating that he had no weapons and was giving up was placed, so the police told the kid to back out of a tool shed he was hiding in. Even though the kid and a friend did everything as instructed and were only holding garden tools, the police proceeded to shoot them both multiple times, sparking an investigation and lawsuits from the families of both kids.

Erin Madden would need an attorney, so I called a good friend of mine who worked for the Cochran firm in Hollywood. He obliged and helped me get Erin a much lighter sentence and lowered the severity of his charges. However, Erin would still do one year at Wayside Correctional Facility and would miss the 2008 football season.

While I was the head coach at Compton College, I was teaching off campus at Sacred Heart High School in Lincoln Heights, a Hispanic-gang-infested part of LA. I loved my time at Sacred Heart. I was the only male on campus, with over three hundred girls, and twenty female teachers and nuns. It was a bit out of my element, but the girls I taught biology to were great young women. I called every single one of my girls within the six classes a day that I taught "genius." They all knew I was fucking with them, but it was a good icebreaker, I thought. I had some troubled

31

girls, and I had some girls with their heads on straight who all had good home lives, but the troubled ones are who I navigated toward. I would help them with lunch money on the daily, they came to me with their problems, and some even got pregnant and were scared to death, but they came to me and told me because they knew I would keep it between us. Due to the fact that I had a daughter basically just a few years younger, I could relate to them all, and they all looked at me as a father figure.

I also taught sex education—yes, sex education to girls. Go figure! I would recruit during my lunch hours, in between my classes, or late at night. I did what I had to do, but it was what I loved. Being a single man at the time, I made pretty good money and was able to get back on my feet. I was paid a salary at the high school and was paid a decent head-coaching stipend at Compton College. Once I was fired at Compton during that 2008 season, I still had the teaching job to keep me afloat, but teaching was not what I wanted to do; it was doing what I had to do.

AIGA Coaching Clinic in 2014 at Long Beach Cabrillo: Steve Sarkisian, along with Tony Dews, Johnny Nansen, Ricky Logo, Kalani Sitake, and Marques Tuiasosopo, hosted by me and George Malauulu.

I told myself that I had to get back into the coaching profession. I ran into a good friend of mine by the name of Kiyoshi Harris at the American Football Coaches Association (AFCA) national coaching convention in Nashville, Tennessee, in January of 2009. He told me they were hiring an offensive coordinator at Chaffey College in Rancho Cucamonga, California. I was introduced to Carl Beach, who was the head coach and athletic director. He was a junior college icon, and he hired me as the offensive coordinator in January of 2009. I will always be grateful to Coach Beach for helping me get my mojo back. He was also a father figure during a rough time and helped me financially as well. Carl was a great man and great football coach.

I would stay at Chaffey for two seasons, helping it get back to its winning ways, leading us to the Western State Bowl in 2010. I was still living in Long Beach. If you don't understand the freeway system in Southern California, Long Beach to Rancho Cucamonga is about fifty miles, but in traffic that is about two and a half hours, so the travel became a bit daunting. I finally resigned from Chaffey College and looked to land something closer to the beach.

With Kiyoshi Harris on the late Tim Valentine's private airplane headed to New Orleans, LA.

33

My next job would be as a head high school football coach at Long Beach Cabrillo. Cabrillo was in the same league as national power Long Beach Poly. So, everyone and their mother told me not to take the job, but Lalo Mendoza, who hired me at Compton College years prior, had a younger brother who was the principal at Cabrillo, and we had known each other a little bit, so I thought it could be a great personal challenge—and a challenge is what it would be. I was inheriting a program that had never been to the playoffs, was a combined 6-54 over a six-year span, and was in one of the most gang-infested areas of Long Beach. A kid was shot and killed just a year prior to my arrival right in front of the school, at the Taco Bell across the street, so peaches and cream this job wasn't. So, I assessed the program and noticed it had some of the best facilities in the area, was in a powerhouse conference in Southern California, the PAC-5, and played the likes of St. John Bosco, Mater Dei, Corona Centennial, San Clemente, Mission Viejo, Santa Margarita, and JSerra, just to name a few.

I wanted to get to work, so that's what I did. My POA at Cabrillo was to make our program and school an attraction for kids to want to transfer into. We did that in a major way. Jumping forward four years, before I left Cabrillo, we had so many transfers checking in at one point that the CIF made a "JB rule"—they actually called it that—to not allow transfers within our own league. They made it so difficult to transfer, and it deterred kids in such a fashion, that the once prominent Moore League is now a laughingstock, and even mighty Long Beach Poly is a middle-of-the-road, average football program. It's a shame. While the private schools flourish and shine, the public inner-city schools suffer and become irrelevant.

The year was 2011 when I accepted the Long Beach Cabrillo High School job. I instilled an early morning breakfast club weight program, which I was told would never work, the kids wouldn't show up, etc. I had 100-percent attendance at 6:00 a.m. for four years straight. Subsequently, we made the playoffs every year I was the coach at Cabrillo. Year one, we had our hands full. I hired a young, energetic staff that didn't know much football, but if they could manage the kids and be on time, I felt it was a win-win situation. I couldn't pay anyone anything but peanuts, which was a small public-school stipend, so I needed some hungry young coaches who wanted to climb the proverbial coaching ladder.

I took a team that was senior heavy to a third-place finish in our league, and our only league losses would be to Long Beach Poly and Lakewood, which both were CIF contenders on a yearly basis. We finished 7-3, which was the best record in school history, so we had made some noise rather quickly.

We went on to build a program and made the playoffs year in and year out, but we could never get over the hump and win a playoff game. My dumb ass built the hardest schedule in America and played the likes of Corona Centennial, St. John Bosco, Orange Lutheran, Villa Park, JSerra, and St. Bonaventure. I had a philosophy, and that philosophy was that if you wanted to be the best, you had to play the best, and you had to play the best before you could ever beat the best, so that is what we did on a yearly basis. Our preseason record was usually not very good, but we finished second in our league behind only Poly the last three years that I was at Cabrillo. We played Poly for the league title twice, losing to them 6-0 in 2013. We had our chances to shock the high school world that night but couldn't quite get it done. I would go on to get a record thirty transfers in 2014, but the CIF and the Moore League fought it tooth and nail and made us jump through hoops. That is what basically ended my run at Cabrillo, and I resigned after the 2014 season.

During my four-year tenure at Long Beach Cabrillo, I never had a taxable income, yet I had a beach condo on the sand and drove a Cadillac. I had to make ends meet by doing odd jobs and running a camp that I had started some years prior, which I called "Pigskin Skills Clinic." I was determined to do what I wanted to do and not what I had to do, so I did it. I helped earn thirteen kids scholarships at Cabrillo; never before in school history had a kid earned a football scholarship. We had kids go to schools such as USC, the University of Washington, San Jose State, Fresno State, and others. I thought we did a good job for what we had to work with, and we changed lives in the community. I owe all the success to Dr. Elio Mendoza, AKA "Doc." Without his support and guidance, Cabrillo would have stayed irrelevant. I told myself that I had to get back to coaching college football. I missed recruiting too much, so I resigned my post at Cabrillo and went to look for another college job immediately.

CHAPTER 3

Ignorance is Life-Threatening

In my opinion, ignorance is truly life-threatening, especially for this new generation, which I believe we have a name for—the millennials, or some shit like that. By the way, it blows my mind that we must name an entire generation! What a bunch of slap dicks we are, and shame on us as parents! I don't believe the kids have changed much. I believe we, as parents, have changed, and we are making our generation soft and enabled. When I was young, there was a list of things that we just couldn't say or do. We couldn't question an adult—ever! We couldn't miss school unless we were dying, we couldn't go outside until we finished our chores, and we had to do our homework every night. We ate everything on our plate, and if we didn't, as my father would tell me, "If you don't eat it, you will wear it." We respected old people, and we went outside and played every day. We were back in the house on time, and we respected girls, or women. We also pulled our pants up, and the rap music, we could actually understand!

Let's take a look at this generation: they don't eat what's on their plates, they don't respect anything, they are the laziest fucks I've ever seen, they question everybody and everything, and they think missing school is the thing to do. But they didn't just come out of the womb thinking these or knowing these things; they were *allowed* to do these things. Furthermore, how can they even think these things that have opened this can of worms? This generation doesn't go outside and play. They sit on their smartphones or play video games hours upon hours, and they don't do any homework. I believe physical education classes in schools have been eliminated for the most part. As kids, PE was our favorite class of the day. Now, these kids have no sense of playing outside, yet we ask ourselves as a society why obesity is at an all-time high!

So, now do you believe ignorance is life-threatening? Well, I do, and I tell parents all the time that they enable their kids. They allow them to get away with any and everything. Until we put our foot in these kids' asses as parents, then there won't be a coach, or a teacher, that can ever teach the youths anything that is worth a shit. It starts and ends with us as parents. Coaching your kids would be so much more fun if we taught them differently. We all would benefit from this, and society may just become that much more enjoyable. I've always preached to my teams that if you see trash, pick it up. If you see an old person who needs help with groceries, help them out. Push in your chairs and pull up your damn pants, but who else is telling them these things? Are we, as coaches, telling our teams this? Contrary to belief, our student-athletes are the most influential students on a campus, and others follow them, but just know that they also follow the student-athletes that aren't being told or taught any of the above mentioned. That is once again ignorance, and it shall be life-threatening.

There are leaders and there are followers in this world we live in. Athletes are always looked to as leaders by non-athletes, and some people have what I like to call an "it" factor. They will be followed by others just because of who they are or what they do on a field or court, and that is powerful shit.

I tell my teams and coaches that we lead others, but the way we lead them is what is most crucial. You can turn right, and they will follow, everyone is happy, and we WIN the game, pass the test, or get the job, but you can also turn left and lead a group to eat the forbidden fruit, which causes cancer within football programs, business offices, or classroom settings. So, we as adults must teach the difference between right and left, and just because you have the "it" factor, that doesn't mean you know how to use it. It's up to us as parents, leaders, adults, coaches, mentors, and teachers to show the way, because these kids only know what they know, or don't know what they don't know, so if we don't show them the way, we are the definition of ignorance and will all have our lives threatened.

I can't stand it when I see grown men, such as NBA, NFL, and MLB players, arguing with referees, yelling at them, showing them up, so on and so forth. It sickens me because the referees just sit there and take it for the most part. The ripple effect is what truly makes coaches like myself motherfuck kids or yell at other coaches who allow it. What I mean by that is this: our young people see how the paid professionals act with referees, or how they talk back to their head coaches or assistants, and, since they make so much money, they usually get away with it. There might only be a few coaches who will discipline a pro athlete, guys like Greg Popovich, Phil Jackson, Bill Parcells, and Bob Knight, guys who have some moxie and who don't give a fuck what popular opinion says. The Brandon Marshalls and Terrell Owens of the world, guys who drop balls on purpose at practice and act fools on TV only make it harder for guys like me, because our kids all want to be like those guys. So, which way do our kids follow? Right or left?

I was always a respectful kid growing up—well, for the most part. I would feel shitty if I saw someone else disrespect a woman or an old person or throw something on the ground for someone else's ass to pick up. It all sickened me, and I vowed to never be that way. I always told myself that if I ever ended up coaching, I would teach these values and the difference between right and wrong. I tell kids all the time that once you grow hair on your nuts and hit puberty, you know the difference between right and wrong, so go to class, sit in the front row, ask questions, take off your fucking headgear in class, stay your ass off the phone, and talk to your teacher after class or during their office hours. I am a true believer of making the teachers work and making them teach you. I was once told by a professor that my kids didn't know how to take notes. I was blown away that a grown person who was so-called educated would say something as stupid as that! I replied by saying, "Well, sir, with all due respect, Jerry Rice didn't know how to catch a fucking football until someone taught him how to."

Ignorance is life-threatening, boy, I tell you. I have always said that if you don't show a kid how to do something, he will never learn it. Teachers and educators make a huge mistake, in my opinion, by writing it on the board or handing out a piece of paper and expecting the kid to learn it, know it, or pass an exam. No, that isn't how our kids learn—well, at least not JUCO kids. Nor do I think inner-city youths learn this way! I believe our kids should be taught in a manner that is conducive to their respective learning style.

I feel that the ignorant lifestyle that we all lead is only going to be handed down from generation to generation as some type of curse, so let's cut it off now, parents, teachers, coaches, and mentors. Let's end this madness and get our youths back on track! People will always evolve and change. The generation now is called the millennials; our next generation may be called the Slap Dicks, if we don't fix these damn kids. So, let that sink in for a bit, especially the next time you as a parent go to your kids' soccer match, baseball game, or football game and dog cuss the coach, yell at the referees, or fight in the stands with each other. This happens, and you all know it does!

Someone once said, "Uncoachable kids become unemployable adults." Well, that very well may be true, but enabling parents create soft-ass kids, and that's a fact! Let's make school and athletics fun, meaningful, and rewarding again, not make it a chore. I'm telling you, many coaches and teachers alike believe teaching and coaching your kids has become a chore, and if you got anything out of the chapter on "doing what you want to do, not what you have to do," then you would know we teach and coach because it's something we want to do. Unfortunately, many of you new-generational parents have made it a job that we don't want to do! Let's fix it and get back on the same page, so we can create employable adults once again.

Coaching is teaching and, vice versa, teachers must be able to coach a kid in the classroom setting as well, because if all coaches just went out and yelled obscenities at kids and didn't teach them shit, then there is no "why you did wrong" and "how to fix it." That is amateurism at its finest, and those people should go find a different line of work. Teachers want to teach a classroom that is attentive and under control, and if there are a few unruly students, then that teacher must be able to coach those particular few and manage the classroom as a whole, but that goes back to having an "it" factor. If you notice, all these things are starting to tie in together.

Ignorance falls on us all and becomes a term that, at some point, we all shall fall victim to. I believe kids are ignorant because they don't know any better, and adults are ignorant because they are stubborn, egotistical, or flat-out defiant. As adults, we do some ignorant shit, and for the most part we understand what we have done and know that is was some foul shit, but when kids do it, they do it because either someone else did it that they looked up to, or they just flat-out don't know better! Ignorance is something we can learn from, but eventually, in my opinion, if we do something once and don't learn from it, and do it again, then shame on us. Then our ignorance has become insanity, because we are now expecting a different result from doing the same shit over and over again. At some point as the adults, we must start setting a precedent for these kids and set the example in stone!

I feel that we have these people from all walks of life—bureaucrats, politicians, presidents, principals, and others—who feel their shit doesn't stink and that they can all walk on water and not get wet. Therefore, our youths look up to these types, because if the people that are supposed to be setting higher standards are doing foul shit, then what are we truly expecting our kids to do? Let's be better, lead by example, and make our kids follow us to the right, not to the left!

The person who says "ignorance is life-threatening" is also very often the ignorant bastard doing the shit he/she says not to do. Let that sink in for a minute.

I resigned my position at Long Beach Cabrillo High School to accept the offensive coordinator position at Garden City Community College in Kansas. I knew the head coach, Jeff Sims. We had known each other for quite some time, but mostly on a casual level. Jeff often came to California to recruit while he was at Florida Atlantic University as the wide receivers coach. When he was at Indiana University as a recruiting assistant for Kevin Wilson, he often called and recruited my kids. We would bullshit, have some drinks, go to a titty bar or two, and that would pretty much be it. I knew once he landed a division-one job, he would be just like the other D-I guys and try to use me for my players and so on and so forth. I knew the business, so since Jeff never crossed me the wrong way, I said, "Fuck it. Why not? Let's go see what this Jayhawk conference is all about."

I had been a California JUCO guy my entire life, so all I knew was Cali football. However, having played my college ball in Kansas, and having a shot with the Chiefs, I had many friends who played in the Jayhawk, and I knew several people in the state of Kansas, so I flew to Garden City for an interview with Jeff Sims in November of 2014 and accepted the job as offensive coordinator at Garden City. I went back home to Long Beach to arrange my move and recruit for Garden City and tried to get the best players I could find.

I arrived on the campus of Garden City on January 2, 2015, and hit the ground running, because if anyone knows anything about Jeff Sims, there is no complacency allowed. You better pin your ears back and go attack the job at hand or you will have no job to attack. I did exactly that. I recruited relentlessly until I signed just about the best class a JUCO could sign in less than two months. When you accept a new position at the college level, you must find new blood, so recruiting is essential. Jeff had a reputation for being a good recruiter, and so did I, so the two of us together landed some big fish, to say the least.

I would try and start working on offense as the so-called offensive coordinator, but that never really happened. It was never actually my offense to call. Everything I tried to implement was shot down by Sims, so, after some time, I was questioning myself as to why I took the job. Was it just to bring this guy a bunch of kids to help his resume, or what? I stuck it out for basically the entire winter and spring. When the start of the summer began, Jeff and I started to rub each other the wrong way, and it became more frequent as we went through summer workouts. We came off the field one fantastic day in 100-degree heat, with the lovely smell in the air of cow shit and dead chickens from the Tyson meatpacking plant down the street. We exchanged words regarding the offense, and I simply said, "You either let me call it, or I leave," so he allowed me to implement the offense over the next two weeks and left me alone.

To make a long story short, we eventually had another war of words coming off the field, which led to a breakfast altercation in the café, and I finally said, "fuck this shit," and resigned immediately. I had brought over a hundred kids to Garden City, so once the kids found out that I had resigned, they boycotted Jeff Sims's called meeting and were at my doorstep some hours later. I was caught off guard, as you can imagine, when I opened my door to 140 players in the parking lot of a shitty apartment complex in Garden City, Kansas. I got the attention of the kids, calmed them down, spoke to them, and told them to stick it out. They needed to make a grown-man decision and finish what they had started! I would take a few kids with me to California as I left, but the other 130-plus kids ended up sticking it out at Garden City. Garden would end up going 3-8 in 2015, but many of the players I recruited who stuck it out would subsequently win a national championship one year later, as all my players matured and performed to greater heights for Jeff Sims.

I, however, had gone back to California, taking a few players with me, as I stated, eventually accepting the Independence Community College head coaching position a few months later. Watch *Last Chance U* on Netflix for the rest of the Jason Brown and Jeff Sims story, if you are wondering what else happened between us.

CHAPTER 4

It Ain't About Me, It's About Us

I truly believe that successful head coaches, successful football programs, along with successful business moguls that run Fortune 500 companies must live by this motto: "It ain't about me, it's about us." I have coached this way for many, many years, and it does two things, in my opinion. It shows your staff, or your assistants in the business world, that you aren't all that matters, that the assistants and frontline folks are who really matter. They are the ones doing the grunt work for your program or your business. I feel that it shows you as a democratic-style leader. Not everything is a dictatorship, although I will have some non-negotiables, or things that I expect to be handled a

particular way or in a particular fashion, but as a unit or program, it's about us at all times.

I see so many coaches who try and dictate every facet of
the program and want everything done this micromanaged way
when, in reality, you aren't on the front line with the kids at
study hall, or breakfast checks, or in classroom checks, or in the
dorms as much as you would like to be, due to all your other
obligations. So, in my opinion, the head coach or CEO should
give some latitude and allow his/her staff to have input and
some suggestions on how certain things can be approached. If
you don't allow for some input, I think you are setting yourself
up for mutiny on the staff, and your soldiers will find it very
easy to walk away or not do what the program requires.

I have a saying I have used with each of my staffs: "It's a
one-tongue language." That means the program requires one
common language to be successful. It doesn't mean become
a dictator and tell your assistants to do shit my way or hit the
highway. It means the entire program revolves around one com-

mon language and set of goals and has one mission statement, so that the program is successful in its totality. I had this motto in my staff war room for years at Indy, and I used it at Compton College as well. It's a good thing to live by as a CEO or head coach, because everyone knows when we WIN, it's a team effort. When we lose, we learn as a unit, and nobody individually lost us the game, or lost us an account, or lost us the sale. So, uniformly, we WIN as a unit at all times.

I used to think it was all about me, that I could call the best play, recruit the best players, and basically thought my shit didn't stink when it came to coaching, but I soon realized it was bigger than myself. It will always be bigger than any coach or CEO that runs or operates a program or business. It's all about the frontline soldiers, so to speak, and the men and women doing the groundwork that we, as head coaches and CEOs, don't have a clue about at times. Coaches are probably the most egotistical group of people on the planet. We all thought at one point that we could control everything, or run everything, and it was a "my way or the highway" type of mentality. But when you do it as long as I have, or as long as many of my mentors or predecessors have done it, you quickly realize that it's a TEAM effort, which means "Together, Everyone, Achieves, More," and I truly believe nobody is bigger than the program or team, and that goes for any business.

I give my entire staff a coaching manual and a job description twice a year: once when I hire them all, and once during the summer when we begin camp. It is very detailed, down to the minute of each day, and it includes each coach's individual duties, so nobody has the same job or task. This allows the staff to work much more efficiently and effectively. I also believe that many hands make light work, and the workload gets distributed evenly amongst the staff, which allows for the program to operate with a one-tongue language, and the totality of the program runs much more smoothly. I feel that this philosophy is what works best for me, but if you read up on the philosophy of a coach, such as Bill Belichick, he will tell you that he believes less is more. I do sometimes tend to believe that, because the more people you have, the personalities multiply, and then you are dealing with a thousand of them at the end of the day.

I feel that winning programs and successful businesses operate with a one-tongue-language approach, where the duties are spread out evenly and, more importantly, they are fair to each assistant, so that nobody feels left out or that they are solely doing too much. You can run into that problem, and if a coach or an assistant feels he/she is carrying a bigger load than other staff members, you can have mutiny in the room. I feel that there is always going to be some things that certain staff members won't or don't understand, and that is why there is a chief and there are Indians. You can't have too many chiefs and not enough Indians amongst your crew.

There will always be a few more seasoned coaches or staff members on your team, but when you delegate duties amongst the staff, some may feel left out or slighted when they get a lighter load. However, in all honesty, the more jobs, tasks, or duties that someone is issued is actually a compliment, not an insult. Many coaches get butt hurt when his or her colleagues get complimented with bigger jobs or a more intricate task within the program. In reality, the one who didn't get the more important job should strive to earn it by handling their own task and doing it to the best of their ability, though, to be honest, their ability may not be good enough. Sometimes, they may never land the big job amongst the staff, and that is just more proof that this is a results-oriented business and that you need the "it" factor in order to be special, in my opinion.

Sometimes in life we need to be thieves and steal other people's traits or qualities, especially within the coaching profession. If someone is a better recruiter than you, then you should learn his recruiting tactics and make them your own. Or if that person is a more organized coach, then you should learn his organizational skills. Never be satisfied with your arsenal. Always look to steal and gather more ammo to increase your firepower and be a more complete coach or a better professional in whatever you do. I think that coaches get caught up in trying to be the person who landed the big recruit, or called the best play, and wants all the credit, yet won't take criticism when he fails. That is often detrimental to coaching staffs and in office settings alike.

We tend to be so egotistical that we try to hide the recruit's information so nobody else on staff can talk to him, or we don't allow the other assistants to help game plan, yet we want all the credit if it succeeds and will be quick to blame the young coaches for lack of preparation. However, you didn't allow it. Remember, we only know what we know, and if we don't help young coaches or staff members learn the basics, then we shall never see them flourish. We want the assistants to do the grunt work and be frontline soldiers, to check classes, do study hall, and check the dorms. Yet, they don't have a say in game planning? This is a cold business and heartless at times, but it's a very rewarding business as well. It's eat or be eaten, and it's a dog-eat-dog world, so earn your stripes, keep grinding, and get your hustle on, but don't ever forget where you come from, and always work with humility and keep your eye on the prize. It's a marathon, not a sprint!

I have never fired a coach; they have either fired themselves or quit, but firing is something that I feel I have never done. Although, on certain staffs of mine, there was an ongoing joke where assistants kept track of how many coaches were fired or quit. It was a very large number, to say the least, but at the end of the day, those coaches quit or fired themselves. I didn't have to fire anyone. They had a job description, and they either didn't meet the standard or weren't competent enough to handle the tasks at hand. I don't go around looking to fire people. I look to help people become better—better players, better coaches, better administrators, and better overall humans. I think that I have done a damn good job of that too! I will give the shirt off my back to one of these kids, or to one of my coaches, but they also can't fuck me or bend me over at the end of the day. I give, but I expect to get your best in return. We teach fundamentals and discipline, but we don't coach effort, and that is a philosophy amongst the staffs that I lead. There will be no coaching effort. Kids owe it to themselves to bust their asses for the team and their futures, but coaching effort is a coaching turnoff, and I won't do it!

My one-tongue language was something I came up with in the streets growing up. You either were on the same page or you were going to jail or getting killed, so we all better have had the same philosophy or been thinking along the same lines. I learned many things in the streets, and later used them in my coaching ideologies, and I truly believe it has made me a better coach. It allowed me to relate better to kids, especially the kids of this generation, and the inner-city youths. I hope more coaches and leaders of men adopt this motto and use it to better serve the people we are in this business for, which are the kids, and helping other human beings along the way. I truly feel that if more people did it this way, we would be much better off when it comes to helping kids, and CEOs would see their businesses flourish as well.

I have seen a lot of coaches come and go, and the one common denominator is work ethic. If you don't have it, you will never work for me or anyone else who has high expectations for their business or their program. I see and hear a lot of bitching with the younger generation, a lot of "give me, give me," but no "earn it, earn it" mentality. Coaches who quit or fire themselves are usually lazy fucks who lean on others to do their jobs or ask others to cover for them while they take a nap. I have seen it all, and the work ethic of these young people in the profession kills me; it truly does. I don't think they understand the reward vs. the risk. I think they all expect the football gods to do their work for them, and on top of that, they think they will be successful in this profession. It blows my fucking mind.

I don't think we understand that the more teeth you cut in this profession, the more blood, sweat, and tears that go into this job, the more rewarding it is! I love it. I think doing shit that others say couldn't be done is the ultimate "fuck you" and the most rewarding aspect of our profession. I think that coaching with the TEAM philosophy is much more rewarding and fun for all involved. You want to keep assistants engaged, allow them to put their fingerprints on the blueprint, if you will. It's architecture at its finest. We have goals, we assess, we build, we create culture, and we are rewarded with the benefits of doing something that everyone told you couldn't be done. Is that not what this is about? We help kids out along the way, which is why we got into this business, so if we are in it for kids, and want the best for them, why dictate a program or business without the full engagement of your staff and assistants? I don't get it!

I believe that it's crucial to set a strong foundation from the very beginning with your staff, well before meeting a single player, or business associate for that matter. The staff must be of the same accord, or what you do with kids is irrelevant, in my opinion. The staff must know your expectations, your do's and don'ts, the job descriptions of each and every staff member, and, like I do, read them out loud in front of the group so each staff member understands what it is that their colleagues have to do as well. I think open communication and being up-front is the only way to go. That way, everyone is working on the one-tongue-language approach, and we are on our way toward the common goal, which is to WIN at everything at all costs!

Christian Villagran, currently the starting QB at Upland High School in California, a very respected program which he led to a 9-1 record last season as a sophomore at my Pig Skin Skills clinic which I ran at Chaffey College for the youth.

Jason Brown

I think that too many head coaches and CEOs simply hand out a plan without the executing format or proper dialogue with staff members, so that the plan isn't properly executed. I feel that a manual and job description is a necessity and should be implemented within all coaching staffs and with CEOs in office settings. I feel the more transparent you are with the staff, the harder they will grind for you and the more loyal they are to your program, but, more importantly, they will be loyal to the one-tongue philosophy and program mission statement.

I feel as if too many assistants and office workers think that being asked to do something or given a task is a slight, and too many assistants take it personally. It's not personal, it's business, and it is what separates winners from losers and successful people from unsuccessful people. It's the driving force that allows our profession to be so different. It allows the blood, sweat, and tears to really matter, and it allows us to truly benefit from the fruits of our labor.

CHAPTER 5

It's a Results-Oriented Business

Midwest Classic Bowl Trophy at NEO, 2017

We either WIN the game, or we lose it. We either sign the recruit, or we don't. We either graduate our kids, or we let them fail. Furthermore, the last time I checked, the game of football has a scoreboard, and at the end of the game there is a winner and there is a loser! There is no gray area in football, and

I am referring to football in its totality. It has so many moving parts that most people don't understand the inner workings of a football program. Any successful program, be it football or a business office, is results-oriented, and you will either get fired or get promoted. That is the harsh reality of this great game and the fine line between winning and losing.

There are winners and losers in everyday life. We just live in a soft-ass generation where everyone receives a trophy, for God's sake. We give trophies for fucking participation! A participation trophy? Are you shitting me? We choose to play a sport, be it recreational or a team sport, and we as parents now expect a trophy for just driving our kid to practice all year? Wow! All I can really say is that it is pretty sad that when I coached high school and we voted for all-league, we literally took five hours to come up with a first team and a second team, because kids who didn't deserve shit were receiving votes just because that kid's coach felt sorry for him, or his mommy was a booster at the school, or his daddy was an alum. Well cry me a fucking river! If your son wasn't any good, maybe you should have pulled him out! I mean, damn, we are setting our kids up for failure and don't even know it!

We have winners and losers in the classroom setting as well, but nobody looks at it like that. We have someone who passes the test and someone who fails the test. We also have someone who teaches taking that test, and if his/her class has over a 50-percent failure rate, I say he/she failed teaching as well. So, there are winners and losers at everything we do, but we close our eyes to it and prefer to wear blindfolds when it comes to reality. I said it before and I'll say it again: there is no gray area in this business. It's results-oriented. If we, as coaches, set goals, if we don't meet them, what do we do about it? What do we say about it? I bet half of us just throw the paper away, start over, prepare for setting new goals for next year, and then do the same ol' shit all over again! That's the definition of insanity! We need to self-assess and ask, why didn't I meet this goal? Why didn't we WIN that game? Why didn't my kids graduate? Why didn't I get one of my assistants a better job? Why didn't

I save that one struggling kid who had the horrible home life? Do that, instead of just throwing that paper with the goals on it away and starting fresh.

I think we, as coaches, sometimes don't want to face the hard truth, because the truth does indeed hurt. However, if you accept the truth and work toward overcoming the harsh realities that the truth brings, then we would all be better for it. Nobody cares at the end of the day. Not one soul cares about you, besides your mother and father, or son and daughter. Besides that, everyone is out for his or her own. Ninety percent of your colleagues would rather see you fall to your knees than see you rise to greater heights, and that is just the truth; but remember, the truth hurts!

I feel that if we would understand failure and have a better understanding that we *are* going to fail at things we attempt in life, then success would be that much more gratifying at the end of the day. Our blood, sweat, and tears would be so much more meaningful, to say the least. We have accepted failure, for the most part, as a society, and especially in our profession, but I'll be damned if I'll accept it. I will keep pushing, keep on keeping on and hustle until I once again rise to great heights and help kids reach their potential—and when I say potential, I mean full potential, not some half-ass moral victory shit either!

I have always told my staff that we either WIN or LOSE the recruiting battle, we either WIN or LOSE in the classroom, we either WIN or LOSE in study hall, we either WIN or LOSE off the field in the community, and usually when you do right six out of the seven days in a week, Fridays or Saturdays usually end up pretty positive! I truly believe that. Winning is a habit, but unfortunately so is losing! I had these types of quotes all over my offices, and I love having everyday reminders up on walls, to visually remind myself as an assistant *what's important now*—WIN.

I think that setting goals is good and all that type of shit, but if you don't hold yourself to those goals as a head coach or CEO, then the results will never be in your favor. If you don't assess yourself quarterly and assess your assistants with exit meetings and evaluations, then you are just going through the motions as a coach and should join the 97 percent of people who just go through the motions and work for the 3 percent of people who don't and get results! If that is what you want to do, then so be it. We all need good assistants, but if you aren't aspiring to have my job and be a head coach, I won't hire you anyway. I believe that the cream rises to the top, that competition breeds hard work, and that hard workers make an average practice a perfect practice, because perfect practice makes perfect, not just practice! Practice means going through the motions and coaches allowing mediocrity, because if you aren't coaching it, you are allowing it! I want perfect practice with instilled game-day situations and vigorous pace with perfect execution. Without that, you are just settling and should go work at the JC Penney warehouse or some shit!

Coaching and teaching require results, as do Fortune 500 companies. Without results, why do we take tests with pass-and-fail grades? Why do we have to meet quotas in the business world, or sell a certain number of cars if you're a car salesman, or several houses if you do real estate? It's all results oriented, and some of us have ice in our veins and attack it. Some of us don't and work for those of us who do have that "it" factor. I have mentioned that several times in this book, and I truly believe successful people have it, and it separates the non-doers and the doers! I'm a doer and always will be. So, ask yourself, what are you? Do you want to work for the doers, or be a doer and help others become a doer?

I give incentives for results; it pushes and motivates people. So, for example, if you land a big-time recruit, I will pay you out of my pocket. If your position group is the most talented amongst our staff, I will pay you. If your group has the highest GPA, I will pay you, and so on and so forth. I believe in incentives, especially for young coaches. It shock treats them into doing something they had no idea how to do, or rewards them if they did something they never believed they could do. Remember, you only know what you know, and don't know what you don't know! So, I give incentives, and I believe it is a great competitive self-motivating tool that pushes assistants to battle each other to get better, stay hungry, and earn results!

I have always pushed coaches to be different, and I execute my plan with a one-tongue language, but I give autonomy to certain coaches who have gained my trust and earned their stripes, so to speak. I'd rather have that coach hate me now and love me when he gets a bigger and better job or can better himself or his family within this great profession. If I am yelling and cussing your ass out, it means I love you and think you can do better or get more results, but if I stop listening to you in meetings and stop cussing your ass out, you should be worried. I may be letting your ass go pretty soon, and if you can't get results, you will be gone sooner than later.

Life is hard and nobody cares. Trust me when I say that nobody cares! So, go be different and get results, because, let me tell you, not everyone in our profession gets results. They are dependent on the hustlers and go-getters on the staff to get results. So, be that guy; don't be the other guy! I always wanted to be "the guy" and not the other guy, but that is me. Who are you? We all need to really look in the mirror and figure these questions out: Who are we? What do we want to become? Why do we do what we do?

It's very easy to be the other guy. It's very hard to be the guy, and that factor alone is what separated me from others and made me who I am today! I wanted to be the head coach. I wanted to run my own shit. I wanted to have the final say. But at the end of the day, I wanted all that to help young coaches in the profession and help kids along the way. I wanted to be the best recruiter in America, and that is what I became. I believe I have the "it" factor as well, so that alone put me in a different classification amongst the coaches in the profession as I climbed the ladder, but that isn't always enough.

It's a "who you know, not what you know" business, and sometimes being rough around the edges, like I am, turned folks off. It doesn't help my employability in this profession, but I said "screw them" and made the D-I coaches need me and my players, because I will always have the best players in America and always will graduate them. So, I will continue to recruit America's best talent, graduate them, and teach them how to be great community members and better human beings. These reasons are why players who leave my programs don't get kicked out of schools at the four-year level!

It's about results. To boast a bit, we broke records at Indy during my tenure. We had 101 student-athletes graduate and sign scholarships to play at the four-year level. We had forty sign to play Division I in 2017-18, which I believe is a national JUCO record. Not only did they graduate, they graduated on time and were at their respective universities for spring ball in January. These are accomplishments that I brag about, not WINs and losses or that we won the conference that season and the school's first bowl game. Who gives a shit? I mean, really. Nobody cares who won a JUCO bowl game. Nobody will even remember it in two or three years, but they will remember the bowl victory at Alabama, Tennessee, Georgia, or Vanderbilt. And how about Arkansas, Washington State, and Colorado? Those victories will be remembered forever.

The bottom line is that without results, without getting those kids recruited to play for me and getting them graduated on time, they would never have those opportunities. So, it starts with me and ends with me when it comes to the classroom, teaching them right from wrong—which they know, by the way. You just have to reinstall it inside their video-game-playing little brains—letting them know there is a pot of gold at the end of the rainbow, but that it will take sacrifice, hard work, and dedication in order to achieve it!

Results are achieved by people who are "different," meaning guys who are willing to do shit others won't do or would never do! That is what different means. Go the extra mile, get to the office before the head coach and other assistants, and stay in the office well after they are gone. That is what different is. You will read about turning over rocks in another chapter, but that means looking for shit in places nobody else thinks of and taking advantage of it. I always told myself and all my assistants that I will sleep when I die. That was my response to all my buddies who told me to go get sleep or get out of the office for a day or two. I always thought that's for the weak-minded individual who has no drive or want in life. I wanted to be different and stand alone when it came to recruiting and finding kids, helping kids, learning offense, being an innovator, doing shit that was said could never be done! That is what I wanted to be, that is who I became, and this is who I am!

I don't live to regret, I don't coach to regret, and I don't regret anything that I have done in this profession. Football is a very special fraternity and is completely different than the business world, but it is similar in the sense that results are what make us different. Results are what get guys paid big money, get us bigger jobs, help us provide nice things for our families, and allow us to live our best life. In saying that, results will never be great if the only reason you wake up is because of an alarm clock! I preach that to my players and coaches. I haven't used an alarm in twenty years. You can ask anyone who knows me, anyone who has worked for me or with me, and they will tell you that I don't use an alarm. I never have and never will. My alarm clock is internal. It's my motivating factor that lies within me to wake up and start over every day.

Bobby Bowden once said in a book that he used to go to sleep at night tossing and turning, just thinking about what it was he could do tomorrow when he got to the office. I have been that exact way my entire life. I used to crave my office at 5:30 a.m., and I might not have left my office until 2:30 a.m., some two and a half hours prior. I loved the fact that I could make myself better, figure out ways to make the program better, and be different, do things that nobody else on staff would do or wanted to do. I would do other people's jobs, not to show them up, but to learn what their job description entailed and be the best coach I could be.

I don't believe young coaches understand that. I truly feel that half of these coaches, even at the D-I level, coach just as a wannabe player would want to wear a jersey on game day to show their friends or girlfriend that they are a part of something. That ain't me, will never be me, and I don't want to associate myself with those types of folks. I want true go-getters and grinders to work with me. I want guys who are hungrier than me—and that's not an easy task. I am starving, and my assistants better be starving as well. I always tell my guys, "I'm not mad at you if you can't do the job at hand, but you can't work for me either, so go find another job in another field, because this isn't for you." But it's not personal. It's strictly business, but people get butt hurt when you tell them the truth, so always be aware of what this job entails: having tough skin, making hard decisions, and overruling the entire staff even when it's the unpopular opinion in the room. That is what being different is and how results are achieved, in my opinion. Just remember that wasn't always popular amongst the staff, and it will never be easy conveying it amongst a bunch of different personalities, but it is what it is.

I don't think General Patton was popular amongst his soldiers, and I am pretty fucking sure he was different than everybody else. He made hard decisions and handed out duties to be executed in a professional manner. But unlike football, or in the business world, people's lives were at stake, so I am sure he lived in a results-oriented business at all times. If he didn't get results, his soldiers died, or we lost battles or wars. I look at shit like that not to compare myself, but to think optimistically that this job is fun, rewarding, and benefits our youths, but without results, we are just wasting peoples' time, our time, and everyone we come into contact with. So, let's be results-oriented, turn over rocks, find what others won't, and be different!

CHAPTER 6

Correction is Not Criticism

I think too many kids nowadays, and young coaches, for that matter, believe that correction is criticism, when in fact it's just coaching and honesty. So, we need to get over our feelings and grow a pair. I've been yelled at, cursed at, screamed at, and grabbed by coaches, and fully accepted it and moved on. I just thought it was a part of coaching and playing football. I never looked at any coach as being an asshole, personally out to get me, or any of that shit. I guess I was cut from a different cloth.

I have had many players of mine get offended by my coaching style, but those players are what we in the business call a JAG (just another guy), but the "Dudes" (real ballers) accepted it, took it as a positive, not a negative, and are very successful to this day. I have twenty-two players currently in the NFL, and

I have sent more than two hundred players to Division I. Out of those two hundred players, not one of them has been kicked out of a four-year institution. So, I do feel that whatever it is I do, or did, has worked, and that is what allows me to sleep at night, not the WINs and losses! To date, out of those two hundred kids, 136 of them have earned their bachelor's degree, and twenty-six of them have earned a master's degree. I will put those statistics up against anyone in this business!

I believe in being a player's coach, someone who has "been there, done that," so to speak. It allows me to relate to today's player. I can reel them back in and gain their trust, which is what this is all about. I was highly criticized for yelling and cussing kids out on Netflix, but what wasn't shown on TV was the time that was put in privately with each of my players, and how the kids knew I wasn't out to fuck them, that I was here for them and always had their best interests at heart.

I do believe in hating me now, loving me at the end when you earn a scholarship. I said it on the show, and I say it again, I don't care about your feelings; this is a results-oriented business, and I am ultimately judged on how many kids I graduate and get to four-year schools. I love this portion of the job, which is helping kids and helping them at more than just football. I like to think that I help them with real-life issues, the daily struggles that we all face. I truly believe you must be a psychologist, meaning each player has a different struggle and a different way of working shit out in their heads, so you better learn your players or you will lose the team sooner rather than later.

I don't ever treat players the same. Each one of them is totally different, and is treated as such. Saying that, I do treat the team the same as a collective unit, which means team rules: discipline, showing up on time, how we operate with a one-tongue language, how we treat women, how we are in the community, our mission statement, our goals. All those things are exactly the same. No one player is bigger than our team, but each player is treated differently by me. I will always believe in this philosophy.

A player such as Rakeem Boyd, who is the starting running back at the University of Arkansas, was treated differently than Emmit Gooden, the defensive tackle at University of Tennessee. They both had some of the same issues, but they were completely different and needed to be approached in a different manner. Delrick Abrams, the starting cornerback at the University of Colorado, was treated totally different than Malik Henry, who is currently the quarterback at the University of Nevada. These guys all needed to be yelled at differently, caressed differently, and talked to in such a way that they each got what they needed from me. Every kid has a different backstory—they all come from a different style of life—so, in my opinion, the head coach needs to learn those backstories and lifestyles so we can help these kids out to the best of our ability.

I have always said that whispering sweet nothings in the ears of today's generation of players will never work; they are too coddled at home. Plus, most kids from single-parent homes are raised by their mothers, and trust and believe me when I tell you that their mothers cuss their asses out much worse than I ever do or did! I believe in tough love and telling these kids the truth, because most coaches or people sucked these kids' dicks growing up and actually took money out of their pockets, but I actually put money in their pockets by giving them the raw and uncut version of reality, and the ones who make it usually listen, have some humility along the way, and allow the process to take precedence.

I call the above-mentioned process a shock treatment of sorts. It is vital to young people that they are shock-treated—meaning, told the vigorous truth about themselves in a manner that only they can understand. This is why I don't deal with parents at the collegiate level; it's not high school anymore. If I spent my time talking to each parent of every kid that I recruit, I wouldn't be able to market each player to four-year schools. I wouldn't be able to help mold these young boys into men. Furthermore, I wouldn't be able to tell these kids in a few years the real world is going to hit you right in the fucking face, so get ready now! I tell most player's parents to call my mom and cry to her. She would cuss your ass out worse than I ever would! I feel that if more coaches took this approach, we would have a much better future generation of student-athletes.

I believe that soft asses make for hard heads—and we have created a culture that has made for some soft asses, let me tell you—but it's not too late, in my opinion, if we all jump on board and start getting our teams and classrooms back under control and all moving in the same direction. I think that we, as coaches and teachers, are great vessels for these young student-athletes and have a huge impact on their lives, so let's not piss it away by not controlling the narrative and using every moment to teach and earn these kids' trust and dedication.

I coached with passion and energy. It didn't matter if I had to yell at a kid or a coach; we were going to get the message across. If I was hated, so be it, but I also got fourteen coaches jobs at the university level, so love me later is fine with me. I will always be judged for everything that I do, now that I have become a public figure, so, although I don't ever regret anything that I did, I do realize now that coaching with a bull's-eye on your chest changes things quite a bit. So, if I want to continue to be used as a vessel for helping kids, I need to be more strategic in my coaching methodologies. We all change over time, and some "asshole coaches" stop cussing, and some "nice-guy coaches" turn asshole. That is the beauty of this profession; we get to adapt and overcome. We will always face adversities in this profession because we are dealing with human beings, young human beings at that! We will always need to adapt and massage these kids in a manner that is conducive to creating a positive culture and assisting these kids in every way that we can.

Criticism is always going to be harsh—that is why we call it criticism—but at the end of the day, if the person giving it truly cares about the kids he is coaching, or the kids he/she is teaching, then it truly is correction, and it's our job to convey it properly. I may be unconventional with my methods, but it's what works for me. You must figure out what works for you, but the one-tongue language and the TEAM concept will allow you to at least have a fighting chance. I loved just about every player that I ever coached or recruited. It's a bond you build, and if you're honest, upfront, and truly have the kid's best interests at heart, that kid will run through a wall for you.

I truly believe that you can cuss a kid out all you want, call them every name in the book, but if they believe you have their best interests at heart and will give them the shirt off your back, then they won't care about that shit; they just want guidance and discipline. Our kids need discipline. They actually require it; they just don't know it. So, it's our job to instill it in them and trick them into learning what discipline truly is. It is what our youths need so they aren't working at McDonald's after high school. Teach them what earning a degree is all about and how it will set their future up for success. I think that we allow too much undisciplined action, and our youths get away with too much, especially if they are a great player. I have been the victim of these types of situations as well, so we all learn on the run, but if we don't correct the mistakes that we make as young coaches, then we are insane, and ignorance is truly life-threatening.

I am most proud of never having a former player of mine kicked out of a four-year school, and that is because my kids bought what I was selling and believed in what I told them. Even with my harsh style and unorthodox manner, my kids always bought into what I was selling, and will continue to do so as long as they know I am genuine and will support them without hesitation. I have always been a player's coach and always had my player's back, but I also told them the truth, what was needed to survive in the streets, and how to "play the game."

I will touch on what I mean by playing the game later in another chapter, but these are all necessities, in my opinion, when coaching and teaching our youths, especially the new generation. I teach our kids to be on time, not to miss anything, sit in the front row of class, and be different, so that the teacher recognizes them in a different fashion. I think most kids are recognized for being different in a negative manner: by being on their phones, being the class clown, or doing shit that isn't conducive to a learning environment. Our kids want to be known for being cool, or being the guy who talks shit to teachers, or who is disruptive in class, because nobody will tell them that they won't make it in life and that this isn't how we operate in a classroom setting or how the real world operates.

We, as coaches and teachers, set our youths up for failure quite often without even knowing why or how we did so. I think that we whisper sweet nothings in their ears and just try to get through the day, so to speak, which is taking money out of our kids' pockets, not putting money in their pockets, as I like to do. I like to put money in their pockets by telling them the fucking truth. Telling a kid to shut the hell up, sit down, and put their cell phone away is teaching them that when they do work at McDonald's making minimum wage, they will be fired for being on their phones, coming to work late, or not getting their job done in a timely fashion.

I teach my kids the importance of earning a degree and not working at McDonald's, teaching them that they will probably work for a person with my skin tone. I tell them: "They don't give a fuck about you! They will fire you for being late, missing work, being on your phone, being rude and disrespectful, and shit like that." So, therefore, I teach them to shut the fuck up, act accordingly, and be respectful so that they don't work some shit job and do what they must do, when they could be doing what they want to do! I think our youths understand tough love and need tough love to get through the harsh realities that life is going to throw at them very soon.

I believe wholeheartedly that correction is not criticism, and if we can convey this to our kids, our profession would be so much better for it. I am hard on my kids and coaches, but it's being different that my guys understand. They understand where I am coming from and what I want. If being an asshole is what it takes to get guys jobs, get kids graduated, and earn them a scholarship, then an asshole is what I will be! I don't care. I don't need them to be my friends, and I don't need kids or coaches to like me. It's not personal; it's business, and a results-oriented business at that!

I will continue to put my best foot forward with kids and coaches alike, and continue to coach these kids up, instill discipline, tell them the truth, and continue to put money in their pockets. I will take the scrutiny and face it head-on, but if I know the truth, my players and coaches know the truth, I will be able to sleep at night! I don't need public opinion to know the truth. They can judge me all they want. I can give two shits about what others think, especially ones who aren't involved in our program or know the inner workings of what we do on a day-to-day basis.

I will keep my eye on the prize, teach our kids to keep their eyes on the prize, and teach the importance of earning a degree and treating people how they want to be treated, and I will continue to mold young boys into men. I will teach the importance of discipline and how to finish what they started, along with getting them where they could not get by themselves!

CHAPTER 7

Playing the Game

"Playing the game" means so much more to me than it probably does to you, but let me explain! I was taught how to play the game at a very young age. The "game" to me equates to life in general: how to survive, how to make money, how to graduate from high school and college, along with surviving the streets of inner-city USA. I will discuss playing the game in this chapter as to how it refers to education and graduation. I am going to discuss some things that you will probably judge me on, but that's okay. It's what I specifically needed to do in order to help others, and it may not be what you will do or what you have done.

Growing up, I spent many days at Compton College and witnessed many unruly things that I won't discuss in this book, but I have seen grown men in the hierarchy change grades for kids, get criminals who were guilty out of jail, and have met crooked judges, policemen, and attorneys at law, but never once did any of that give me the right to judge someone or understand the inner workings of what it was I was witnessing. I didn't understand what it was that I had witnessed until many years later, and I am very proud of myself for not being the judgmental crybaby-ass kid that many of my friends I grew up with were. I just stayed in my lane and kept my fucking mouth shut, as my father always told me to do.

I am who I am because of my youthful days, and it has allowed me to help numerous kids that I have encountered and save numerous lives. I wouldn't have had it any other way. I am proud of who I am and what I have done. I have taught all my kids how to "play the game," and that game would prove to save lives and help hundreds. I believe education is a money-making scheme that gives out a piece of paper after you spend tons of money and learn absolutely shit! I couldn't tell you one fucking thing that I learned in high school. I could *possibly* tell you a handful of things that I learned in college, yet I hold four degrees and am working on a fifth via an online program.

I am dead-ass serious when I say these things. Education is a game, and I teach my players how to play it! I didn't attend many classes while I was in junior college, let me just be honest, but I learned that this school shit was a game and that I needed to learn how to play it—and play it I did indeed. I think I may have attended four classes in two years in JUCO, but still earned my associate's degree with just under a 3.0 GPA. So, pardon me when I say education is a mockery and a huge scam. Our college athletes make billions of dollars for these schools, only to be left with student loans, bills, and injuries from playing a collision sport—which, by the way, allows the institutions to build libraries, computer labs, tutoring centers, and pay coaches millions of dollars. I think it's a joke and a slap in the face of every kid that plays in the NCAA who doesn't get paid, who performs for that school and simply puts money in all the politicians' and bureaucrats' pockets on a year-to-year basis.

What happens to that kid if he/she suffers a career-ending injury? Does the NCAA pay him/her? Fuck no! Does the university pay them? Fuck no! They just thank them with a letter every year—oh, by the way, they then have the audacity to ask for money as an alum. It's fucking sad. Let me just tell you, I have seen and heard it all, and all I can do is continue to push forward, stay the course with my kids, and teach them what this game is about and how to play it. That is all I can really do, because most people my players cross paths with will take money from them, not put money in their pockets. That is the sad truth and, sadly enough, it will be the kids' closest friends or family that will want the most.

I have witnessed grades change in administrative offices just to get that kid eligible to play that week. I've seen it all, and when your program has the highest enrolled group of kids on a campus, it is what pays those instructors at the small commuter schools, such as JUCOs and learning academies across this country. So, that is what I did. I got the teachers paid by filling their classes with kids. FTE (full-time enrollment) is a term that colleges love to hear. When you have the most full-time-enrolled kids on a campus, you have some wiggle room to play the game. I played it because, at the end of the day, if we teach our kids to go to class, sit in the front row, take off their headgear, stay the fuck off the phones, and turn in some homework, they will pass with a C. If they pass a test and go talk to the instructor during his/her office hours, there's a high probability that he/she will earn a B in that class, so play the game!

I was once told by an instructor at Independence Community College that my players didn't know how to take notes, so they would never pass his class. My mind was blown away. I was in shock. I couldn't believe what came out of this grown man's mouth, someone who was a so-called professor at a college.

I simply replied by saying this: "Tom Brady didn't know how to throw a football, either, until someone fucking taught him how to. You must be shitting me; you will fail a kid because this inner-city kid who couldn't even read at a third-grade level didn't know how to take notes?"

I then simply asked this man this question: "Did you turn down Harvard to be here at Independence Community College?"

He replied, "No, sir, I didn't."

So, then I said, "No shit. I didn't turn down USC to be here at Indy either. And by the way, my kid who can't take notes didn't turn down Harvard to be here either, so how about we teach them how to take fucking notes!"

It blows my mind how ignorant some grown folks are and how people expect kids to know what they don't know! We all know what we know; it's that simple. It's a process that we need to teach—and teach is what I did when it comes to playing the game. I argue this topic with everyone, and people tell me all the time, "Well, your player can't read."

I respond by saying, "No shit. But teach him to be a good kid, love on him, and get him to the field on game day, and guess what? I bet you his ass can sign an NFL contract on signing day! I know that much!"

Who am I to judge a person on his/her intellect? This life isn't built on intellect; it's built on being a good person and being trustworthy and loyal! That is what it's built on, so let's teach great football players to be great humans, and then they will be put in a position to better themselves, their families, and their community. I truly believe that. I think that too many people put too much stock in passing some politically correct test or exam and not taking proper notes for something that we will never use again in our lives. If we put more stock into teaching our kids to be better humans, have more respect, and tell them the truth, we would be so much better for it.

I demanded that my players sit in the front row at Compton College. I didn't allow hats, hoodies, or headphones, and they couldn't be on their cell phones; that was in 2007–08. I did the exact same thing at Indy from 2016–19, and I got the same results. What results were those, you ask? Well, leading our conferences in team GPA multiple times, graduating more student-athletes than any other school during my tenure, and earning more kids D-I scholarships than anyone in America. That is what the results were—and by the way, we live in a results-oriented business! My coaches didn't like checking classes three times a day, or doing study hall, or checking dorm rooms nightly, but it's part of the job that we accepted, and it's most definitely the single most rewarding thing in life! Watching a young person walk across a stage with his/her diploma/degree, and not having to visit him/her behind bars or attend his/her funeral, is why I teach young people how to play the game!

I have seen over twenty of my former players sign NFL contracts, and many of them couldn't read at a third-grade level. I won't mention names, but trust me, I used to read books to my players at 5:00 a.m. when I picked them up from home to take them to school. We did in-house tutoring as best we could. That is why I always hired coaches who had master's degrees, so in study hall we not only controlled the session, but taught the kids what they needed to learn. I was always ahead of the game, and that was simply to keep my kids ahead of the game, because *if you stay ready, you ain't gotta get ready,* and I truly believe that! We live in hard times, especially for our inner-city youths, and so many people take advantage of these young boys and girls. I'm tired of it, so let's teach our kids how to play the game and be better people for it.

This game I talk about is a cold one. Trust me when I tell you, it's colder than the dope game, but at the end of the day, the more we teach our young people on how to play it, the better our future generations will become. I truly believe that what I learned in the streets, and what I found out about school and the educational system, has helped me help others. Without knowledge we are nothing, but knowledge isn't always learned in a classroom! Life is a hands-on, experience-based training session, and without the harsh realities that life throws our way, we wouldn't be shit in this world. The four pieces of paper that I possess that say Jason Brown has earned the above-mentioned degree are all bullshit. I earned my life by learning how to play the game, and playing the game is what life is all about!

CHAPTER 8

Slap Dicks, Shit Birds, and Fuck Sticks

I want to clarify some shit in this chapter. I will define each word specifically within this chapter, but I want you all to know that I don't recommend every coach call their kids these words, because you have to earn the right first and foremost, and secondly, they must believe in you in order for you to call them these fine names that I like to refer to as "slap dicks," "shit birds," and "fuck sticks."

I have called kids all three of these names as a coach. Even when I was a young coach coming up the ranks, I would call good kids "slap dicks." It's just a term we use in the profession, but I would be the guy who was known for changing the way we used these great words with kids, and I think it has followed me everywhere I have been. Slap dick has been a football coaching term for as long as I have been alive, and I'm sure Coach Lombardi used it, as well as Bill Parcells and many other coaching legends, so I take no credit for such a word. I guess the context in which I use the words has given me some notoriety.

A slap dick is basically any player on the team, and he can be called a slap dick for just about anything at any given time. A slap dick, often shortened with the word "slappy," can be used for kids who miss a class and couldn't wake up, a kid who was late to a meeting, or a kid who got caught cheating on a test, but all these above-mentioned items being totally out of this particular kid's character, he would then be called a "slap dick." I would then call that kid in and ask him what the hell was going on, that this wasn't the kid I recruited, and so on and so forth. He would apologize and tell me he had a bad week, or that his mom was struggling at home and he couldn't study, and did a bonehead move by cheating on an exam, or something along those lines. I would give him a punishment, as I would with anyone, and we would be on good terms once again, but that kid had earned the term "slap dick," and he would be called that for his remaining time under my watch. A slap dick was the kid who you loved with all your heart and had athletic ability, but couldn't run the right route to save his life, or wouldn't line up correctly on defense if you drew it on his visor for him, but he would run through a wall for you and always have a smile on his face; that is a true slap dick. Those types are the slap dicks we all coach this game for.

I mentioned that a slap dick is a kid who missed his first class, cheated on a test uncharacteristically, or possibly missed a meeting or was late to practice, but once those things became more frequent and that kid became a repeat offender, his ass would now become what I like to call a "fuck stick." A fuck stick is a kid who is usually a follower and tries a little too hard to be cool, someone who wants some attention amongst his teammates. That is the kid we want to break sooner rather than later. If that kid isn't broken, he will turn left and become a "shit bird," which I will discuss here shortly. A fuck stick is a kid you can massage a bit and get him back to slap dick status, but he is at the crossroads and will either turn right or left, as mentioned in previous discussions. I have had several of these so-called fuck sticks, kids we would like to save, and if we could just save one, then maybe this could be the one!

Fuck sticks are kids who only know what they know and have never been told the truth by any grown person. He/she could be someone who just wants to test the coach or try you. A fuck stick is usually a good player, but they could become a cancer within your program, and then you will eventually be left with a decision to either cut this cancer out or let it grow amongst the crew. I have had several of these types, and they either will "shit or get off the pot," so it's our job to get them to where they can't get themselves. I think that it's a fine line between a slap dick and a fuck stick, and it could be one decision that can turn that kid into either one. I think that a fuck stick needs a bit more "motherfucking," so to speak, and we as coaches need to be a bit more of a hard-ass on these types. A slap dick can be either cussed at or nurtured, but it's that "it" factor that helps you figure which one is needed.

Slap dicks can become fuck sticks overnight, but a "shit bird" is a kid who usually is broken and on a short leash with me. A shit bird is usually damaged goods 99.9 percent of the time and cannot be fixed, no matter how great a player he is. The shit birds will be your most talented players, no question about it, but if you coach with the philosophy that no one player is bigger than your program, then you will most likely cut this cancer out before the spreading begins. Shit birds usually come to your program from another program, or two other programs, sometimes even three programs, so that should be red flag number one. Red flag number two is his backstory at home, what his/her home life is like. You can usually put the pieces of the puzzle together rather quickly with shit birds.

Shit birds are usually the kid who says all the right things to your young assistant coaches, or says a bunch of sweet shit to his/her teachers, and the teachers call you and tell you how

Jason Brown

much they love this shit bird, but in reality this shit bird will end up fucking your entire program over if you allow it—and if we aren't correcting it, we are allowing it! It's very simple. Don't let this fake-ass kid pull an okeydokey on you. I have had some real shit birds throughout my coaching career, but remember, when you are a true go-getter and great recruiter, you will land some shit birds. That's just the nature of the business, and that's what makes this profession so beautiful, in my opinion. It's how you handle them that defines your season, in my opinion. If you allow them to permeate and influence your good kids, then you will have the slap dick kids turn into fuck sticks, and the fuck sticks will all become shit birds, and the shit birds will kill your program and the team. Shit birds are liars and thieves, and they

76

are usually the ones selling the weed to all the fuck sticks on the team. The slap dicks are the ones who fuck up and try to smoke at a party one night and get caught, and now you have a few bad apples ruining the entire bunch.

As a coach, you want to save the slap dicks, and even a few fuck sticks, but I have learned over time that the shit birds can't be saved. I have possibly saved one true shit bird, and that was a sales job by me, which was done just to benefit our program. Unfortunately, that kid is now in jail, and I feel that I fucked that kid by not cutting him and telling him the truth, but I was a young coach and thought I could save them all! Once again, you cannot save them all, but we better save the ones who need saving and want to be saved. Once you coach a few years, you will be able to tell who the ones are that need saving, and the ones who can't be saved, but you will need the "it" factor to determine these types of things.

My definition of these three often-used terms may vary amongst you and your staff, but make no mistake about it, these terms are real in our profession and are used in a variety of different ways. I just wanted to clarify the differences between the three. These definitions are my own, and I'm sure you will have your own, so let's all use them in a manner that is most effective to get through to our respective kids. I hope you can all coach up a slap dick, save a fuck stick, possibly save a shit bird's life, and help them understand that there are more important things in life, and just maybe we can all be better for it.

77

CHAPTER 9

Turning Over Rocks

"Turning over rocks" is a term I use when I refer to recruiting and getting shit done! This business we all call football is results-oriented, so turning over rocks is an essential piece within this profession. When I say turn over rocks, it's not a complicated term to grasp. It requires hard work, dedication, and determination. With these three things, all is possible within our profession, and turning over rocks is just a small piece of the puzzle when it comes to achieving results. If I was defined as a coach, I would say that I am known as a master motivator, great recruiter, and an innovator.

I came up with a four-point plan when it comes to recruiting. It is as follows:

Find: We can all find someone, be it on social media, through a friend, or via an online notification through a media outlet.

Locate: But can you locate them? Where are they at? Not so easy!

Contact: Finding them and locating them is easy, but can you contact them? This is the hardest aspect of the four. (This is truly turning over rocks!)

Recruit/sign: Can you land the big fish, sign the kid, and get him to your school or program?

If you cannot turn over rocks, you won't even find someone, let alone contact them.

When I address assistants and give them a job description or issue duties to be completed, I expect them to turn over rocks

MY TEAM IS ALWAYS HUNGRY

to complete a lot of that shit. I will always have the assistant who comes to me or to a meeting and says, "I didn't find it" or "I was told he wasn't available" or "he won't make it" or "I'm still waiting for him to call me back." It's all bullshit! In this results-oriented business in which we live in, you either get the result or you don't! I truly believe it and will always believe it, because once I hear that shit from my assistants, I immediately go to see if it's in fact true, and when I get the kid on the phone, or if I get the kid to complete his FAFSA (financial aid form), or if I get the kid to do whatever the fuck it is my assistant couldn't get done, I consider that to be a teachable moment, and it's crucial for young coaches to see it and learn it. I may be an asshole throughout the process of teaching it, but they will understand that turning over rocks is essential and not for the lazy-fuck coach, but for the determined one, the one who is dedicated to perfecting his/her craft!

Turning over rocks is as vital to our profession as the kids we coach are. Without turning over rocks, we would never find

the Akeem Ayers or Brad Sorensens of the world, and, therefore, we would never be in a position to help one of these great
kids mature and graduate onto bigger and better things. We all
have been assistants, and when I was one, I would try and turn
over rocks in the ultimate fashion, by handling shit I wasn't
even supposed to do, and when the head coach asked me for
it, I immediately handed it to him. That is why I came to work
before everyone else and left after everyone else. I turned over
every fucking rock I could in between those times. If a recruit
became available, I wanted to be the guy who found him, who
contacted him, and who landed him! If I didn't get that done, I
felt like a loser. I'd feel like I let down my brothers in the office,
and it would piss me off so badly that I would not only turn over
rocks, but would turn over fucking boulders if I had to in order
to find the best fucking recruits in the nation.

I don't think a lot of coaches nowadays understand the
true definition of turning over rocks, and they have become
complacent in the workplace and allowed mediocrity to set in.
Therefore, the Indians don't work for the chiefs in an efficient
manner, allowing the program to suffer setbacks, which allows
other programs to become better than yours. I used to have the
term "Turning Over Rocks" all over our recruiting boards and
made sure it was seen daily, a constant reminder of how to beat
our opponents on a day-to-day basis.

I believe complacency is a coach killer, and a program killer
to boot, so it should never be allowed in offices. If I witnessed
complacency, it would boil my blood and piss me off to where
I often called staff meetings to discuss it. "Discuss" may not
be the proper word to use here, but the staff would know that
complacency wasn't going to be allowed in my program. Ever!

In college football, recruiting is our lifeblood. Even in high
school football nowadays, recruiting has begun at the middle-
school levels; high school coaches go recruit them. So, if it's
our lifeblood, how can we become complacent? I ask my staff
these types of things quite often, and when I hire a coach, I
give him the definition of what the word "recruit" means. If he
can't define the word over time, then I usually get rid of him,

because recruiting is what makes or breaks us as coaches, and, not to offend anyone reading this book, but players WIN games, coaches lose them, and I will die believing that statement!

When I was an assistant, I used to love when other assistants said, "Fuck that kid. He is a shit bird. Let's cut him and coach up the other guy." That was always a classic line from the guy who couldn't recruit a whore in a brothel, but in actuality that coach just couldn't: (A) manage the kid or (B) relate to the kid. The obvious factor is that he didn't recruit the kid, so therefore he felt no obligation to him. So, I would be the asshole on the staff who would tell that particular coach what I thought about him and his coaching. I would eventually be the guy on staff that nobody liked, and I quickly learned that this business is eat or be eaten, and I was going to eat!

I knew in my heart that those assistants couldn't turn over a pebble, let alone a rock, so they would always settle and be that complacent asshole we all despise. I told myself and my close friends that I never wanted to be that guy. I wanted to be the guy who turned over rocks, landed big fish, and worked relentlessly with a great tenacity. I wanted to be the guy who had an unparalleled drive for success, someone who wouldn't be matched regarding my work ethic. I often heard assistants use every excuse in the book. So, as a coach, I just hate hearing excuses. As we all know, excuses are like assholes: everyone has one!

As a player, I never once missed a practice, a meeting, a weight room session, or anything else for that matter. Even when my father passed away, I was at practice coaching that afternoon! It's the job I accepted, and as a player, it's the game we chose to play. So I think it's weak-minded to miss or be late to anything job or game related. I hear kids say they "love" football all the time, but in theory, they don't love it or they wouldn't miss anything that was required of them. I hate when I hear that from a kid who just missed a class or weights, or when an assistant coach says he will do it after he finishes this or that. When I cuss their asses out for missing something, or for them telling me some excuse, or when I tell that coach, "Shit, my bad, I forgot to pay you this month," I tell my story of coaching the day my dad died, how it's what we chose to do, and if you don't want to have both of your feet in this job, then go do something else. An excuse wasn't going to work with me—not now, not ever!

I don't know if people understand that this is never personal and it's all business, but when you take money off my table by not doing your job, then I have a problem with it. You have basically made your decision by not turning over rocks and choosing to be complacent in a results-oriented business. I have heard every fucking excuse in the book, and it sickens me to watch coach after coach just sit back and accept these shitty-ass excuses, when truthfully we should be holding these kids responsible for their actions and teaching them, once again, that the real world is going to hit them in the mouth very soon, and if they don't get their shit together, they will be another statistic in this cold-ass world. So, figure shit out, stop being complacent, and turn over rocks!

CHAPTER 10

Hustler

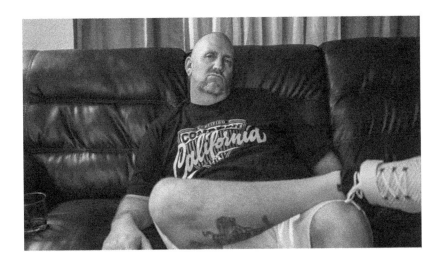

A stone-cold hustler is what I am, and doing what I wanted to do is what I did! I could have done what I had to do, which was work a nine-to-five job at some random place of employment, or figured out shit and coached football like I wanted to do! I don't feel that I am understood from the documentary on Netflix, but if you read this chapter, it will shed some light on the real coach JB.

I grew up having very few Caucasian friends, and I probably can count on my fingers how many I have now. But, having said that, I am very well versed and consider myself to be a chameleon of sorts. I can blend in wherever I go, and I can be around any crowd, no matter what city it is in. There is street code, one of those codes being "real recognizes real," and we know the look of a man or can judge character using our intuition. I have a black daughter, and when I was in public places with her mother, I would beg people to look at me crazy or say something slick, because real does recognize real, and they probably would have had their teeth smacked in for talking shit, but that never happened. When someone did say something smart, I was quite the knucklehead, but that was years ago, and I'm a different man now.

I am the most laid-back person you will ever meet, but if crossed I have a severe temper. That temper led me to some bad places in life, but I am thankful that I was able to get back on track and regain my focus. I had a daughter, took her to college with me at a very young age, played football, went to class, didn't smoke weed or do drugs, raised my daughter, and graduated with a degree.

I could have easily gone the other way, turned left at the intersection of life, and been writing this book from behind bars or some other institution. I tell my players that type of shit every day, and when young coaches ask me what it was like growing up in Compton as the only white boy, I tell them that it was great, that was my home, my people, and nobody judged me. I was part of the neighborhood, and I was never looked at any differently.

I got the "it" factor from my days growing up in Compton, because, without it, I would be dead or behind bars. I had to be a chameleon to understand where I was, what I was a part of, what it was I wanted to be known for, and how I was going to survive the mean streets of Compton, California, in the 1980s. I never thought that I was an outcast or someone who had to look over his shoulder. I walked home with my friend's mother and older sisters. They taught me how to stretch out a dollar and turn it into five by simply teaching me how to, for instance, buy a bunch of candy from the wholesale market at three cents apiece and sell them for twenty-five cents apiece. Little shit like that added up to a kid who had nothing. They taught me how to hustle and survive in the streets, especially during a very hard time. Being the only white boy was challenging, to say the least. These are all things that a classroom could never give me and will never give you! I truly believe that the streets raised me, and the circumstances it presented me with are what allowed me to be the survivor I am to this day.

I would go on "missions" as a youngster with older folks who taught me how to blend in and how to "walk the walk, and talk the talk," how to not stick out like a sore thumb, and how to be different! I was ten or eleven years old at this time; they were eighteen, nineteen, and twenty years old, so growing up I always hung out with the older folks. I consider myself different in so many ways—not that other people aren't different, but I feel like I grew up in a unique situation. I had two older brothers: one I stay in touch with somewhat, and one whom I have no clue about. They also grew up in Compton some ten years prior to me, but they didn't hang out with the neighborhood folks, and they didn't want to learn the culture or listen to the streets like I did. I wanted to learn it. I wanted to be it, and I quickly figured out that the common white person, other than my mom and dad, were totally not like me, nor did I want to be like them!

My grandparents' home is where I spent most of my time, until the day my father passed away. I was there helping them out, taking my grandma to the hospital to have tests run, or taking her to the California Department of Motor Vehicles to simply get her license reissued, even though she was approaching ninety years old—she simply wanted to tell people she had a license, which I thought at sixteen was admirable, to say the least. I saw shit growing up, such as guys being shot close range on the front yard of my grandmother's house, people being chased down and shot in the back at the dead end of our street, and friends having their heads blown off at house parties.

In 1992, on a Friday night after one of our high school football games, we went to our friend's liquor store. His parents owned it, but he would work it on weekends, so we would go in and buy drinks and just bullshit around. We liked people-watching on weekends in there because of all the different characters who would walk in. But on that somber evening, I witnessed a robbery and murder in cold blood.

My friend and I were minding our own business when a couple of guys walked in with ski masks on and grabbed my friend at gunpoint. While he held my friend, he demanded that the owner, who was our other friend standing behind bulletproof glass, open the door and give them the money in the cash register. My friend couldn't do it, so he slid some money under the glass for them. As the assailants grabbed the money, they shot my friend in the head and proceeded to run out like the fucking cowards that they were. My friend's brain matter, pieces of his skull and tissue, splattered all over my clothes. I was literally in shock for a few minutes as I tried to hold myself together. The police, who heard the shots, came running in and found my friend convulsing on the ground. It was too late: he was pronounced dead at the scene.

That was shit that I wish I had never seen, but I am also grateful that I witnessed something that taught me not to be at the wrong place at the wrong time! I had shit happen that I wouldn't wish upon anyone. The street life isn't for everyone. The weak get stomped on and run over, and the strong barely survive, so hard work, dedication, and determination are what allowed me to survive and make it out alive. I am grateful, and now I can help others see what I couldn't see at the same age. I feel as if I was placed in the positions I've been placed in to help others as a vessel, as I said before. I love helping folks, and good-hearted is what I am, but don't cross my ass; it won't be nice. That's just the mentality that I had as a youngster, and it's the mentality that has put food on my plate for forty-three years.

I grew up with a bunch of hustlers, dope dealers, pimps, gangsters, and just about any law-breaking citizen that existed during the time. I love them all for allowing me to see how the real world operates, how all people have choices, and how the choices we make are what define us as humans. I could have steered wrong many times. I had plenty of opportunity to do so, but I chose to not smoke weed, not do drugs, not pimp females, and be different! I think the weak-minded individual is someone who blames everyone for their shortcomings and cries a river to everyone that "it wasn't their fault," or "I could have done better," or "if this would've happened, I would have been this or that." I sum that up by calling them weak-minded fucks who blame everyone because they were a follower and not a leader like I wanted to be. I never allowed myself to follow another motherfucker, and it was not very hard to have weed thrown in my face or be in the dope game, but I wanted to be an athlete and serve in other ways!

I wanted to help others see that there is a way out, a better life to be had, but it would take perseverance and determination. Life isn't easy. If it was, we would all be handed the fucking winning lotto numbers! We aren't handed the winning numbers and must earn every inch of this life, but when you finally make it and overcome the obstacles that life will throw your way, it will be that much sweeter! There is no more rewarding feeling in life than to accomplish something that someone else said couldn't be accomplished, and I loved being the underdog! I embraced it; I attacked it with a tenacious mindset that nobody was going to defeat me, and nobody was going to get me caught up doing something stupid!

My upbringing has allowed me to help so many young kids. I have kept kids from going to jail, being killed, and taught them how to raise a child, but what I cannot give them is the "want to." They must *want* to make it out to better their lives, help their mothers, provide a better home for their children, and do and have the things that we didn't when growing up. I believe people that I come across have always bought what I have sold—meaning that whatever it was I preached, it was well received. Most people bought it, and hopefully it saved someone's life!

I want to make you understand that hustling isn't doing shit that is illegal, it's figuring out life and making ends meet as you do what you want to do, not what you *have* to do! I want you all to understand this point, because it's a rare drive that lies within special people, and special people are who we need more of, so we can affect our youths and get them to where they can't get themselves. I truly believe my statement, and without being a hustler, I wouldn't have been on a Netflix show, nor would I be writing this book. So, figure out your hustle and do what you want to do!

I had a kid at Indy named Kailon Davis. He had two siblings die in just under six months. He was going to head home and give up school and football. I had to convince him to stay and do this for his own child and his mother. His sister passed away, and it would have been very easy for him to just pack his shit and leave, but he bought what I sold, and he has now accepted a full scholarship to Arkansas State University. Those are the stories that allow me to sleep at night. Fuck winning football games; it's a gratifying moment that lasts about thirty fucking seconds. It's shit, means nothing to me. The life encounters that occur are what allow me to breathe new life and allow me to coach college football.

There are over two hundred kids I have earned scholarships for, twenty-plus kids playing in the NFL (six of whom won Super Bowl rings), and former players earning Pro Bowl honors, but that means nothing without the hundreds of success stories and the struggles behind the scenes that allowed the story to have such a sweet ending! Life will throw you curveballs, and I would want it no other way. It toughens your skin, builds character. The cream rises to the top, so not all of us will make it, but the ones who do either listened to someone who had

their best interests at heart, or they simply wanted it more than everyone else!

I like to remind people that there are a ton of success stories, but without the failures in my life, I wouldn't be enjoying any of the success. I tell folks all the time that for every Kobe Bryant or Michael Jordan, there were ten other guys who were better than they are who didn't make it out the hood. For every Lawrence Taylor or Joe Montana, there were twenty guys who were better that couldn't get out of their own way and make it out the hood!

It's a sad reality that ends with a great reward. Learn from others' mistakes, listen to the wise, and persevere and stay determined in whatever it is you choose to do! You will always be judged, so keep your head down, eyes up, and do what others say couldn't be done! "Hustle until you make it" has always been my motto, and doing what others told me couldn't be done is what motivates me to this day! I am being counted out by many as I write this book, and it's okay with me. I love the shit. I will always be okay and make shit happen. I will also make shit happen for the ones who I have yet to encounter, the ones who I can't wait to help, and the ones who only know what they know and don't know what they don't know. I will always strive to be the best JB I can be, and I will always hustle at what it is I want to do.

CHAPTER 11

Coaching is Overrated

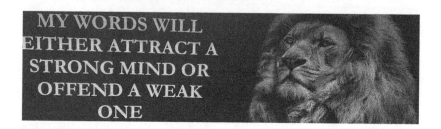

MY WORDS WILL EITHER ATTRACT A STRONG MIND OR OFFEND A WEAK ONE

I truly believe that coaching is overrated and that players WIN games. Coaches lose them! I will stand by this statement for as long as I coach. As coaches, we are the most egotistical creatures on earth, and we all think our shit don't stink, so it's truly funny to watch coaches think it's because of them that we WIN or lose the game. In this chapter, I will discuss the true importance of the coach and how we are overrated, but also how a good coach can give the great players guidance and teach them how to WIN. I will also discuss the truth, which is that the best players WIN games, and it's not even questionable.

When pushed to the limits as players, we find out how important football truly is to us. We figure out very quickly if this is something that we want to do long term, or if it's just something that is for social status and just to be the cool guy on campus. Therefore, we coach so that we can see the cream rise to the top. The definition of the word "coach" is to "get someone to where they couldn't get themselves," so it's our job to recruit the best players, get them to do right and go to class, act accordingly in the community, and practice every day to WIN on game day! That is what coaches are for. We teach the nuances to our players and push them to the limits, so they can figure out that football is just a game and should be fun, but discipline is what separates the good teams from the great teams.

Bad players don't take much seriously. Average players only take games seriously. Good players take practice and games seriously. Great players take weights, conditioning, practice, class, and games seriously! It's our job to get average players to do the right thing daily, get the good players to be the leaders, and get the great players to the field on game days! Just get them to the field; it's that simple. Teach them, coach them, tell them the truth, be hard on them, show them tough love, set the tone, and, oh yeah, get rid of the fucking bad players!

That is a great recipe for success, and if you set a standard and follow it to the letter, you will have a culture, and that culture will be what separates your program from the others. Let me tell you, less than 20 percent of programs hold the players to the highest of standards; most allow more than they don't allow. So, if you don't allow the bullshit, and stop the spread of the cancer, success shall follow.

It's the little things that get you beat on game day. It's not the Xs and Os, it's the Jimmys and Joes. That is an old football saying amongst coaches that I truly believe in. It's about getting the players to run through a wall for you. No matter what play is called, no matter what odds you are up against, and no matter how tall the feat seems to be, it's all possible with trust, belief, and perseverance, along with some hard work and determination, sprinkled with some dedication and a true love for this great game we all love!

While at Indy, I was asked how I came up with such big-time play calls in crucial situations, and I responded by saying this: "I called a fucking dive play just to get out of the first half. Rakeem Boyd is just better than everyone else on the football field and went ninety-nine yards." What a fucking play call by me, huh?

I have always found it funny to be tabbed this great play caller as I was coming up the coaching ranks. In all reality, I just had better players than our opponent had, and I taught them how to act right, go to class, do right in our community, and be good

93

Some will understand this and some will not....

THE DISTANCE
BETWEEN
WINNING &
LOSING

human beings; the rest took care of itself. I truly mean that. If you can get your program to do right six out of the seven days in a week, you will usually WIN on game day! I think if your players act right in the community, go to class, stay off their cell phones, ask questions, clean their rooms up at night, be on time to everything that is required of them, and practice hard, game day will take care of itself.

I believe that quite too often, as coaches, we allow our best players to get away with shit. So, on game day, his teammates don't trust him/her, or they simply don't want to go to war with a person that looks for shortcuts, someone who is late when everyone else is on time, or a kid who misses class when the rule states that we don't miss class. Those are all recipes for disaster and will cause your program to deflate sooner rather than later. Sure, you may beat the shitty teams simply because you have better players, but when you face the disciplined, hard-nosed teams, your true character will be tested, and it will come down to players who are better because they know how to be good people all week long and do the little things, such as touching the line during sprints, or finishing all the way through the line as we condition. Those are the things that separate winning from losing.

I have watched many coaches promise kids shit just to get them to the field. Well, once you tell one kid, you have told them all. That's why you can never trust one. Treat the *team* the same, individuals differently, and be honest, because at the end of the day, if there is no trust in that locker room, your program is shit and you will have too many Indians and not enough chiefs! There needs to be order, regardless of whether you are a player's coach or a dictator-style of coach. The order needs to have one tongue. Everyone must be on the same page, or you are just coaching to say that you have a whistle dangling from your neck and that you wear a headphone looking cute on a sideline. Be a teacher! In this profession, that is a lost trait. I wish more of us taught the kids instead of just watching the kids do stupid shit! If we aren't coaching it, we are allowing it! Remember that.

You may have heard me on the documentary say that if kids run through a wall for you, then you will probably have a good team. Well, that shit is nothing short of the truth. I should get that statement patented! If kids trust you, believe in you, and have your back, then they will do what nobody else thought they could do, which is break that tackle, recover that fumble, or score that touchdown in the waning moments of that crucial game! I could call peanut butter and jelly as an offensive play call, and my players who believed in me as their coach and as a person would run through the wall and score a touchdown on a

Jason Brown

fucking play we called peanut butter and jelly! That is real, and that is what many of us don't understand. Coaching is overrated, and we put too much stock into it. Have fun, be disciplined, and tell our kids the truth. Make them buy what you are selling and watch them run through a fucking wall for you!

CHAPTER 12

Every Day is an Interview

Every day is an interview. That is what I tell every player that I come across and every coach who has ever worked with me. I truly believe it, because someone is always watching you, regardless if you know it or not. Along with that, I believe first impressions are very important, especially when applying or interviewing for a job, so my mindset works in such a manner that I go into that interview on edge, never too confident and always humble.

I think the way we dress, the way we talk, and our mannerisms are all a part of preparing for whatever it is that we do in life. If someone is always watching us, why not always be prepared? If you stay ready, you ain't gotta get ready. That is about as true as true can get! I feel that a prepared mind doesn't have to guess about anything, which equals success, in my opinion. In football, we as coaches have a saying: "The eye in the sky don't lie." Well that goes for us as coaches, or businessmen/

women, executives at ESPN, you name it. We all are being watched. So, therefore, every day is an interview, and if we walk the walk and talk the talk, we can at least stay one step ahead of the so-called eyes in the sky.

I have been told that I will never land a D-I job because of how I dress, my haircut, my rough-around-the-edges personality, and my lifestyle, but when it comes to pure principle and beliefs, I just can't change for someone that I do not know. Therefore, I never changed the way I dressed, my haircut, or how I am with kids. It's who I am, and many of you may say, "Ignorance is life-threatening." Well, yes indeed it is, but if kissing ass and doing shit that I don't believe in is ignorance, then ignorant is what I am!

I have always had the best players. I have always graduated them faster than any other coach in this game. So, therefore, pretty much every coach in America knows who I am, and I know them, but I have yet to be offered a full-time D-I job, and at the end of the day, the D-I coach needs me; I don't need them. So shit, maybe I will just start charging these fuckers like a street agent or some shit! Who knows, but what I will tell you is that I do right by my kids, my coaches, and I will always preach to folks that every day is an interview, and that just because I say something, it don't mean that you go and do it! "Do as I say, not as I do" is an old saying, and I live by that as well. Some folks are just better suited for jobs that they do well, and maybe, just maybe, JUCO is my calling. Due to the fact that I truly believe JUCO is the single most rewarding level of football, just maybe I will stick around at this level for a while.

People always ask me why I am so hard on my kids and coaches. Well, to answer that question fairly, it's because every day is an interview, and nobody cares at the end of the day. Everyone wants results, because we live in a results-oriented business. Therefore, I push my guys to the limits so that my kids who do go D-I don't get kicked out of the school or expelled for dumb shit, because they understand what it takes to get up at 5:00 a.m. for weights or practice and sit in the front row of class and act accordingly with instructors. Furthermore, my kids don't go to jail when they leave me either. Say what you want about me, but I give my kids harsh reality talks on a daily basis—I tell them the truth, not some bullshit lies just to have them play for me and use them like a piece of meat in a meat market like so many others do. My kids understand hard work, how to act right, be good men in the community, and how to treat women, which all equates to being interviewed every day, and they understand the eyes in the sky don't lie!

When I was the head coach at Compton College and Long Beach Cabrillo, I made my kids wear a shirt and tie to games. Our coaches also dressed nice, and we all understood that every day is an interview and that game days are no different. It's a business trip, and we should all dress accordingly. I have a huge pet peeve as a coach, which is talking on a fucking bus traveling to a game. I can't stand it, and I usually lose my shit with coaches first, for not controlling the group, and the kids second. However, after I went to the shirt-and-tie model, I have had fewer disruptions and more focus, and, when we get off that bus, we are usually ready for action.

I had some good friends of mine tell me real interview stories, and one stuck out in particular. Todd Littlejohn, who is a current coach at Prairie View A&M, was once interviewed at the University of Michigan and was doing a great job, until the head coach at the time came from behind a screen and asked him a bunch of football-related questions. He sort of froze up, and the sweat became evident as it ran down his face. He swallowed more frequently and became a bit nervous. Coach Littlejohn has coached at places such as USC, Cal, Syracuse, Buffalo, and New Mexico State, and he realized every day is an interview. The moral of this story is that we should always control the narrative and control the interview, because once we let it control us, we have no shot at the job! So, be prepared and show confidence, and jobs will come your way.

I believe in teaching my players and young coaches that every day is an interview, and I have had several coaches I got D-I jobs for call me and thank me for preparing them like a professional, because at that level, the eyes in the sky are much

larger and interviews are much more scrutinized. I try and prep all my guys, and just because I don't do the shit, it don't mean I don't know how and won't teach it. Do as I say, not as I do! Every day is an interview, and don't ever forget it!

CHAPTER 13

Indy's Last Chance

Let's get this underway. DreamU is what I called it, and the Pirate revolution began. As I smoked a cigar on my beach-house deck in Long Beach, California, one October afternoon in 2015, I received a phone call from a person at Independence Community College in Kansas. I had resigned a few months prior from Garden City Community College in Kansas and was doing nothing but reformatting my resume. This was basically the first downtime I had had in over twenty years as a player and coach.

As I sit and write this book, that time reminds me of my current situation, as I am having some downtime after resigning from Indy earlier this year. I overlook a different beach on the Pacific Ocean, this time being in San Diego. As I sit here sipping a margarita and writing down my thoughts, I look back at what I built at Indy. To the many of you reading this, I understand that I may come off as an arrogant person, but professionally I am as humble as they get, and anyone who truly knows me will tell you that bragging about myself is something that I do not do. However, as I think of my days at Indy, all I can really say is: "Fuck! What a ride!"

I didn't know where Independence, Kansas, was. I had resigned from Garden before ever coaching in a single game in the Jayhawk Conference, so I was still a bit unfamiliar with the location of a few of the schools and their proximity to Garden City. Even though I traveled the state of Kansas quite often to recruit and knew most of the locations, I had never been to Independence. I was invited out for an interview around Thanksgiving of 2015. I caught a flight to Wichita, where I rented a car and drove the two-hour hike to Independence, but instead of staying in Indy that evening, I stayed with my old coach and mentor at Fort Hays State, Jeff Leiker, who subsequently became the athletic director at Indy's archrival, Coffeyville Community College. I stayed the night with Coach Leiker, and we bullshitted a bit about the conference and just shot the shit like the good old days at Fort Hays State when I played for him.

I woke up the next day, thanked Coach and his wife for their hospitality, and drove the fifteen minutes to Independence, where I would meet my future boss, Ms. Tammie Romstad, formerly Tammie Geldenhuys, who happened to be a Kansas State Hall of Fame basketball player. Her jersey hangs from the rafters in Manhattan, Kansas, in the K-State gymnasium. My first impression of this lady was that she "got it." She understood what it was going to take to turn a program around that had a mere four wins in five seasons and eight wins in ten seasons. This was going to be a complete overhaul, and overhauling shit is what I do best!

The interview lasted for about ten hours. Tammie put me through a very intense and thorough interview that day, and I thought it was very good. Interviews are priceless, in my opinion, regardless if you land the job or not. My advice is to take as many interviews as you possibly can within this profession. The interview Tammie put me through that day was one of the best I had ever been associated with, and I had been through quite a few. I thought it was well thought out, very organized, and it involved all departments on campus, so the entire campus knew who I was.

I felt as if I had hit it off with the boosters, donors, and administration, but truly there was only one person I wanted to impress, and that was Tammie. I thought we understood each other and both wanted the same things, which was to set a culture, recruit quality student-athletes to Indy, and get them graduated—along with winning a few games along the way, of course. I flew back to California, waited a few days as Tammie wrapped up other interviews for the call to offer me the position.

I received that call from Tammie one December evening in 2015. After working out a few travel details, I gladly accepted the position. I would pack up some belongings, jump in my Cadillac, and take the twenty-four-hour drive to Indy. I began immediately, and my first order of business was to interview a few holdover coaches from the previous staff. I knew that I was going to call the offense and didn't need the offensive coordinator, and I knew I would probably coach the QBs, so I didn't need the QB coach, so I informed both of them that I would be moving in a different direction.

The only kid I kept was a coach by the name of VanDyke Jones. He showed up in a suit and presented himself very well. He was an African-American man, and I knew that this job, and JUCO jobs in general, require some young energetic black male role models for the inner-city youths that I was about to recruit. So, I hired VanDyke and we both began to implement my plan of attack.

The first official hire I made was my defensive coordinator, who was a coach by the name of Jason Martin. I had pushed Jeff Sims to hire him at Garden City with me a year prior. We had some history, both being from California, and I knew his older brother, Demetrice Martin, who had been a former California JUCO coach himself and has had coaching stints at the University of Washington, USC, UCLA, and now is currently the defensive backs coach at the University of Arizona. I liked Jason's pedigree and his work ethic. I felt he could recruit and would be loyal, so I reached out and offered him the job. Jason then made the drive from Garden City to Indy, which is about six hours across the state.

We began to rip apart the facilities, or what we called the facilities at that time. We knocked down walls, carried out brick, painted buildings, had carpet and tile put in, created office spaces, and started fundraising for a weight room, which Indy did not have at the time. I loved every minute of it. I love rebuilding programs and doing what others say cannot be done. As I reflect on the hire of VanDyke Sennia Jones II, I have a saying that you read in the chapter before this one: "Every day is an interview." When he came to interview with me in a suit, I felt he understood first impressions, and I liked his spirit, but I knew he would have some things to figure out, and being a young man in this profession, I felt he would be a good assistant.

I have always hired guys using my gut instinct, and this staff would be hired no differently. So, as I continued to turn over rocks and explore assistant coaching possibilities, I wanted

We took an old outdoor basketball court and turned it into a fantastic weight room, thanks to Mama Pirate herself, Judy Harris.

to hire young, energetic guys I could somewhat trust and who weren't afraid to get their hands dirty. I found quite a few during the winter months, but only some of them made it through to spring. This job isn't for everyone, and not all coaches understand what a true grind is, so working with me probably isn't the easiest thing to do as a young, wet-behind-the-ears assistant coach, but, like I say, hate me now, love me at the end when you get a job.

I had helped eleven coaches get D-I jobs before arriving at Indy, and, at the end of the day, that is what being a head coach is all about. I helped ten coaches here at Indy get four-year jobs, bumping up my total as a head coach to over twenty. I have always used a motto within my programs: Educate, Matriculate,

Bob Craig is in the white shirt. I called him Bob the Builder. I owe this man everything. He created the facilities that you now see at Indy!

and Graduate. That goes for my coaches as well. My assistant coaches are held responsible for everything that they do within a program, but the head coach is held accountable for the entire program and its inner workings.

As we continued to build in the early winter months, recruiting would be top priority, so I sent Coach Martin on the road, and we set out to put Indy on the map! I needed a catchphrase of sorts to attract talent and let everyone know Indy was ready to compete nationally, that we weren't going to settle for mediocrity. I came up with DREAMU, hoping it would resonate with the high school kids that we would recruit on Twitter. I wanted to kill social media, because that is how the kids communicate today. I made it mandatory that all staff members create a DREAMU Twitter and Instagram page, along with Facebook, so that we could attack from all angles when it came to social media. We ended up trending on Twitter, so we did a great job reaching out on social media, and we caught fire!

We had an out-of-state limit our first year at Indy, so we had to recruit the state of Kansas hard and heavy. We did indeed hit it hard, as I did at Garden City the year before. I had strong ties from my playing days at Fort Hays State University. A lot of my former teammates were now administrators, coaches, and even some principals. I had a good rapport with most of them, and they were willing to send me their players from previously built relationships. I was a good teammate in college, and many of my teammates are still my friends to this day. Although I am from California and not Kansas, I have strong feelings for my Kansans. Kansas was good to me, and I will always have good things to say about the people there.

We had quality Kansas kids, combined with twenty good out-of-state kids, which I must admit was fun and exciting. We had fun as a team. Our staff worked hard and recruited throughout the year, which this job entails. Recruiting is our lifeblood, and we did it better than anyone in America during my tenure at Indy. We built a weight room, coaches' offices, and a locker room during that first season at Indy. There was a lot of blood, sweat, and tears that went into that first year, but I wouldn't have changed a thing. It wouldn't have been possible without the support of Tammie, who had a vision that was equal to mine and would often remind me that Rome wasn't built in a day, even though I often disagreed with her. I am probably the most impatient person that I know, and for an athletic director, I was probably hard to work with at times, but Tammie handled me greatly, and I am forever grateful to her for that.

Tammie gave me everything that was needed as a coach to build and operate in a successful fashion. I met with her one eventful afternoon to explain the fact that we didn't own a sled, we didn't have cones, nor did we have pop-up dummies or a five-man sled for the offensive and defensive lines to practice with. Tammie responded by telling me she had never been asked for these things, so it never crossed her mind to purchase any. I said I understood, and we went on to make our program as good as we could with limited resources. Indy was known as a basketball school, having won a few national championships back in the seventies and eighties. Football was not important, and the town had few expectations of it. I wanted to change that and create a culture that would be conducive to winning. Let the building begin!

We went on to have a great signing class in 2016, with the likes of Jonathan Banks, who would go on to have a stellar career at Tulane University. A transfer from Kansas State University, Jonathan was from Houston, Texas, and a great leader. He was one of my most favorite kids to ever coach. Jonathan's biggest attribute was that he was a winner, and he willed us to five victories in our first season, with victories over Butler, Coffeyville, Hutchinson, and Highland, which, combined, was a first in over thirty years.

Jason Brown

New Weight Room

Locker Room

Jason Brown

New Team Meeting Room and Film Rooms

Many Hands Make Light Work

We had built the foundation for what we wanted to stand for. We didn't have the best facilities, but we made it very comfortable to operate and work in daily. I worked my staff harder than I worked the kids, so I wanted nice offices and decent facilities for them to operate in every day. We never stopped building. I would often tell Tammie, "Once we stop building, we will never catch up with the Joneses." We built and built until we became nationally known as DREAMU!

We had a good nucleus and group of kids our first year. We worked hard and we bought into the program and our community. It was probably my most fun as the head coach at Indy. I also brought a few players with me from Garden City, including a Wichita native, who played at East High School, by the name of Dominic Webb. He was a good kid who didn't like it at Garden, so he transferred to Indy with me. Dominic was a gutty performer who lacked overall height and size, but he had heart and was a good team guy. I also brought one other QB with me from Garden who I had recruited to from Miami, Florida, by the name of Alin Edouard, a former Syracuse signee out of high school. Alin had a big-time arm, could run like a deer, and was probably the single highest-character kid I have ever been around. Alin would sign with the University of Texas at San Antonio after that season.

We went on to have the first winning season in over ten years, along with earning over thirty kids scholarships; several signed with Division-I programs. Leading that class was Jonathan Banks, who signed with Tulane. Ben Knox, our left tackle, signed with Colorado State University, and several other players went on to sign at four-year institutions. We had a very successful first campaign at Indy, and it would be a stepping-stone to bigger and better things.

As we entered the 2017 spring, we had a motto, WIN, as I previously explained, but in 2017, I changed that to "Expect to WIN." Expectations were at an all-time high. We recruited with relentless effort as a staff, and results are what we earned that second off-season. We had a great signing class, and the good freshmen that we had signed our first season had matured and bought into our program. I thought we had a good chance to WIN a national championship that season, and we approached it with that mindset. We had a pretty good nucleus, but when you bring in a high number of big-time recruits, you will also have some headaches. It takes a special staff to massage those recruits and mold them into winners. In the spring of 2017, the out-of-state limit was lifted, so we now operated under a new rule.

We recruited every swinging dick that we could. We signed twenty-eight D-I transfers. Eighteen of them were former Power-5 recruits, and on paper we were as talented as any JUCO I had ever been a part of or had seen. We were long and athletic, we could run to the football, and we had playmakers all over the field. We had Malik Henry, who came from Florida State University, enroll that January. Malik and I had prior history, being that we were both from Southern California and shared the same mentor, Cornell Ward. I thought we had a legit shot at winning it all. We faced adversity that spring, as any JUCO does. We had our dorm issues, we had our issues with marijuana and the occasional drinking disturbances, but we had no arrests, nobody was thrown in jail, and the team came together by the time spring ball ended.

I called for a spring recruiting staff meeting to go over some details regarding recruiting and our spring plan as we wrapped up our own spring ball. I received a phone call during that meeting from a California number. As I would with most unknown numbers, I let it go to voicemail. Once that meeting ended, I listened to the voicemail. It happened to be a lady from the critically acclaimed Netflix series, *Last Chance U*. I wanted no part of it. So, once I listened to the message, I immediately called a staff meeting. We met again, and my staff glared at me with curiosity as to why I had called a meeting ten minutes after ending one. I explained the nature of the call that I had received and if they had any suggestions or thoughts. I usually took advice from a few more-experienced, trusted coaches of mine, and that is what I did that afternoon.

I went around the room asking for input. Coach Martin, who always had good ideas, said, "Why not?"

I said, "Why not what?"

"Why not do it?" he replied.

I said that I didn't know much about *Last Chance U*, but what I did know was that I didn't want a microphone on my person all day and night. The camera I could give two squirts about, but that fucking mic was my major concern. I had only watched

115

maybe two episodes of the first season at East Mississippi, so, although I thought it was a good concept and represented JUCO, I didn't really want to be on it.

I slept on it and called a few people that I look up to in the profession. After careful consideration, I told my staff, "Why not? Who am I to not allow young coaches and players to be marketed on a very popular Netflix series?" So, that is what I did. I called the nice lady back and told her we would be interested, and the rest is history!

Greg Whiteley and his crew arrived for our spring football game that year, observed us, interviewed us, and used his gut instinct, as I often do when recruiting players and hiring coaches. Greg seemed to be a stand-up guy and good person. I met with him several times over a two-day span. We hit it off, I thought, and immediately thought they were going to choose us for the next season.

A few months passed, and as we entered summer workouts, I received a phone call from Greg that we were his choice to film. So, after meeting with our president and with Tammie, we gladly accepted the role of being the new *Last Chance U*.

Just a few big-time signees during my tenure at Indy. DREAMU, baby!

That summer flew by, and Greg's crew of cameramen and photographers rolled into Indy and were welcomed with what I think was somewhat open arms. I believe that most of our campus accepted them. Most of the younger people in town accepted them, but the older folks wanted nothing to do with them, nor did our governing board of trustees. I thought, "Wow, why wouldn't a town of just over nine thousand people want the notoriety and marketability that Netflix could offer?" We had a horrible marketing person at Indy; marketing was nonexistent. The school that I inherited was behind the times, to say the least. We needed resources, we needed support from the town, and we needed a legit booster club that would raise us some funds.

I met some great people during my time in Indy, some very supportive donors who had some pretty good money who offered to help me build, and to whom I will forever be grateful. The Oaks and Hugos, to name a couple, helped us build a turf football field in the spring and summer of 2018, which is probably the nicest turf practice facility in all of JUCO. It still pisses me off that I had to leave that behind. It was a great talent attraction and could have been a huge benefit to the program if I were still there.

I had to get used to the cameras in my face and the mics being placed on me every day, but after the first few days, it was just the norm, and I never really thought about it again. The crew filmed everything, both meaningful and meaningless hours of film, just to capture what ends up being eight hours of footage. I loved those guys. They did a great job, were fun to be around, and were a part of Indy history. They were a part of our program, and we called them Pirates, just as everyone on our team was called Pirates. I will always hold those guys dear to my heart, and I still talk to them to this day.

The filming never stopped, and we went into our first game with high hopes and high expectations. We were ranked for the first time in over ten years and were going to face a team who had recently been in national championship games, won their conference several years in a row, and had a great program over-all. Iowa Western would be a formidable opponent, but the big-

gest opponent that warm Saturday evening would be the lights, camera, and action of the Netflix crew and us. The moment was too big for a program that just had its first winning season in over ten years and still was learning how to become a winning program. It all fell on my shoulders. There was no doubt that we were the more talented team that night, but the better team beat our asses and gave us some humble pie, to say the least.

I would evaluate myself and the staff the next day. After putting some thought into it, I told myself that there was nothing to change; we just weren't ready for the hype and needed to just relax and play ball. Playing ball is what we did, winning seven games in a row before losing a heartbreaker to a Butler County program. We would win the Jayhawk conference the very next week vs. our archrival, the Coffeyville Red Ravens, in front of a packed home crowd. It would be the first conference championship in over thirty years for Indy, and we would go on to earn a berth in the Midwest Bowl against Northeast Oklahoma in Oklahoma. We went in ranked number six in the country, and after we defeated NEO for the school's first bowl victory in the history of Independence, we climbed to number four and would end the season as the highest ranked Indy team ever!

As we entered 2018, we continued to recruit with relentless effort and build what I thought would be another national championship contending team. The show aired that July, and the rest is history. Many think that it's by far the best *Last Chance U* series to date and one of the most entertaining shows on Netflix. I have yet to watch the entire series, and probably won't do so. However, I will never forget the time we put in together that season and how rewarding it was.

Greg Whiteley contacted me as we wrapped up the season and said they would like to come back again, so would we accept them back? I told Greg that I thought he was a great human, and I would love to have them back, even though I knew they had yet to capture a national championship on their show. I wanted to be the first. The crew would soon be back to Indy, and we gladly accepted them with open arms as a staff and as a team, but I am unsure to this day if the town had fully

119

accepted them or how grateful the town was to have had over a hundred million sets of eyeballs on them. I think many were ungrateful, and I thought that the townsfolk could have shown much more love than they did. Indy will forever be known now, and the money the show made Independence was far more than they could have ever expected. I couldn't control any of that nonsense, so I stayed in my lane and continued to work.

I met some amazing people along the way: actors, entertainers, the shout-out from Charlie Wilson on Twitter, along with Michael Rappaport's Halloween-costume imitation of me, and so on and so forth.

I would say it has been one hell of a ride. I only wish the next season had been more productive on the field, but what

INDEPENCENCE CC FOOTBALL 2017-18 SIGNEES

INDEPENCENCE CC FOOTBALL 2018-19 SIGNEES

We had over one hundred players sign scholarships and move on! I can sleep at night knowing we did right by these kids.

can I say? JUCO is JUCO, and sometimes you have too many bad apples that ruin the rest of the batch. I continued to love my players and coaches, and we finished off *Last Chance U* Season Four in style by winning an overtime thriller vs. Ellsworth.

I thought by at least finishing the season on a high note that it would catapult us into 2019. I truly believe we arrived in 2019 on a high note, and I felt nothing but positive energy. I thought we had a great staff and some good character players, along with a very talented group.

To make a long story short, we had a dismal 2018 campaign, and I feel that we all got a bit complacent and had some bad character on our team. I think knowing the show was coming back brought out some bad character, and everyone wanted to be a fucking actor! I went into the 2019 season with a completely new mindset, which was "CHARACTER 1st." I had it wrapped all over the walls of the weight room and in the locker rooms. Just about anywhere I could wrap a graphic, I did.

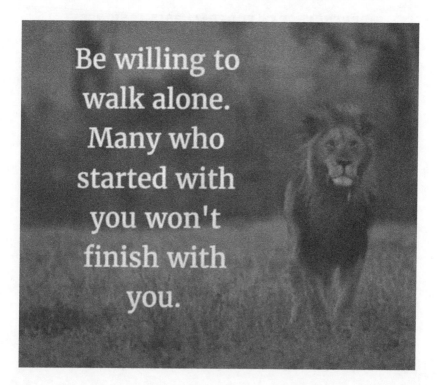

How my Indy run ends will be told in the next chapter. I will always be fond of the people in Indy and how they treated my mother and me when she came to visit. I have the utmost respect for the many people who assisted me in Indy, and I can't express how I feel for them, but all great things come to an end, and that time had come for me. I am proud of our accomplishments. I say *our*, not mine, because it is truly about us, not about me. We sent more kids to college on scholarship than any other school in America during my tenure, and I am proud to be a part of that. I thank every coach who ever worked with me and every player who came through our program. I thank the folks in Independence who accepted me and opened their arms up to my players and staff. I also thank the many fans and supporters who have followed me and supported me during this process. You guys mean more than you know! Much love!

CHAPTER 14

Live and Learn

I NEVER LOSE. EITHER I WIN OR I LEARN.

I never lose. I WIN or I learn. That is what I tell my team on a regular basis, and I truly believe in it. The statement has power, it has truth, and it's a belief that I have regarding life in general. I have fucked up quite a bit in life, as have we all, but it's how I responded to those fuckups that defines me. I believe we are all defined by how we react to setbacks and how we overcome those trials and tribulations. I believe college football is its own sorority, so to speak. It's a private fraternity that should be treated as sacred to all who have either coached it or played it. I have said shit to kids that has offended people all over the world, but what you don't know is that I never had malicious intent or tried to offend anyone during the process.

I have always had a rhyme and reason to my coaching tactics, and it's my upbringing that I owe that to. I believe in relating to all walks of life, being a person who wears his heart on his sleeve and wants to genuinely help others. I have always been this way, and my players leave my programs knowing I had their back and always loved on them. I cared about the person, not the player—and not only that person, but his/her family and what was going on in their lives. I am a recruiter, so in being the best recruiter I can be, I had to learn more about that kid than just how fast he was or what his favorite football team was. I had to learn about his life, his goals, what he wanted to be in life, and what his mother did for a living. Those things are what makes our great game beautiful and is why I coach it.

I don't live with regrets. I have done some things that I look back at and wish I could have done differently and resent, but never do I say I regret this or regret that. If I lived that way, I couldn't coach and mentor young people, because coaching requires love and hate, and it's the valleys and peaks within it that make it special. If you think that it's going to be all glitter and gold, you are fooling yourself and should change career paths. I was fired at Compton College during my first college head coaching job, I resigned at Garden City, and I left Indy with zero regrets. I made the choices during those particular times in my life that, sure, I resent some shit, but I don't go around sulking in regret.

I am human, just as is anyone else who has made mistakes, but what kills me is that people judge me for what they see on a show or how I run my program. I find it funny, because it would take away from my job if I critiqued others or judged them on how they performed their jobs. I truly don't understand how people can judge a public figure but not have one fucking clue how the profession truly operates or what lies beneath the blood,

125

sweat, and tears of this great profession. I don't understand how people find the time to talk shit about another person when they should be finding the time to improve their damn selves.

I am perfectly fine with being judged. I understand that I am a public figure now, and the show will forever be a part of me, but the real Coach JB is someone you should really get to know before truly judging me or how I operate. We have all done stupid shit, and we have all done great things in life. We have helped others and we have hurt others, but that is called life, and in life we are going to have some hiccups along the path we travel. As I always say, which way are we going to turn when we come to the stop sign? Right or left? That is the most important aspect of our true character and how we should be judged.

I never lied to a kid or a coach, and I never will. I have always been transparent with my rants and raves. I am always going to be the same person. I never have been that guy who was inconsistent or the person who staff always wondered whether would show up to the office that day. I think that being truthful and letting guys know where they stand is the key. It at least lets people know your thoughts, so guys know how to work around it better. I felt that if I could do that, it would help

My folks.

me be a better leader. I would learn new things every day. I tried to pick the brains of people who ran successful businesses, or read books from successful coaches, not specifically football coaches either. John Wooden is one of my favorite coaches of all time. I used many of his quotes and methodologies. I also pay attention to Geno Auriemma, because anyone who can WIN as much as he does and manage women the way he does, I figure is someone I should take an interest in.

Learning never stops and *should* never stop. We should always learn, because our kids change. If we aren't on top of the trends and how these kids function, we shouldn't coach. I will always be innovative with my teachings, and I will always look for new ways to coach, but one thing that I will never do is lie. I was once told by a wise man, my grandfather, "Once you lie, you have to make up another lie to cover up that first lie." Then you become what is called a liar, and there is nothing worse than a liar and a thief, and those are two things I didn't want to be. The things I harped on with my players were don't lie and don't steal. Be honest and everything else will fall into place.

I resigned at Indy in late February, 2019. However, on my birthday the week prior, there was a board meeting to discuss a text message that was sent to a manager who I had allowed to be a part of our program. This particular kid was a foreign exchange student from Germany. As the 2018 season came to an end, he would come by and tell me how badly he wanted to play football and be a part of something special, so I told him if he would help me around the office as we approached Christmas break, when we came back from break to start the 2019 offseason, I would allow him to participate.

We came back from break and I had hired new coaches and recruited new players, so it was going to be hard for this kid to crack our lineup, but I kept my word and allowed him to participate. I met with him and informed him that he would be held to the same standards as everyone else on the team. He would have to work his ass off in order to make our spring roster. This kid often called himself "Hitler," referring to the ruler of Germany who ordered the murder of many innocent people. He often

Family

walked the halls with his hand held high in front of his head as the German Nazis did, so I brought his ass into the office to tell him to quit that shit or he wouldn't be a part of my program any longer. He stopped and continued to work out with us, until he broke my "conduct detrimental to the team" contract and had reached the allotted amount of points that I allowed. I brought him into my office and suspended him until further notice.

He was obviously disappointed when he left my office, as he then proceeded to head up to the academic buildings where classes were being held and cursed out some kids and teachers in his German dialect, which was the final straw for me. I cut him from our team via text message. It's possibly something I shouldn't have done, but when you coach 150 other kids and work every day to make each of them better, it's hard to bring in the same kid over and over and expect him to take you seriously after he has proven his worth. I cut him, and he proceeded to go tell my boss, Tammie, and President Dan Barwick, who counseled him and told him to stay away from the program for the time being. I then received a call from an instructor that he was showing off a particular book, Hitler's autobiography, *Mein Kampf,* which he proceeded to put on his social media. He later deleted it, of course, but once I saw it, I texted him to bring his ass to my office and that I was his new Hitler. It was between us, common talk, and he often joked with me quite frequently. I texted that because of the book that I had just been informed about. Because President Barwick is Jewish and this kid was representing my program, I felt obligated to try and save the kid, so I texted him that, simply to show him I was his coach and he was a kid who needed some fucking help. Little did I know that I had so many haters on campus that a grown person took that text and baited the kid to turn it over to just about every media outlet known to man.

If you watched the show and know anything about me, you probably have figured out that I didn't give a fuck about him telling someone that I texted him that. Never in a million years would I think something as sacred as a football locker room and a tightly knit sport such as football would include a kid who

snitched on his coach or tell a lie such as he went on to tell. It's funny how shit works out, because a coach I had fired some weeks prior to all of this also took this kid's side and would eventually bash me on social media as well. This person I just called a coach was actually me being nice, because he was never a coach; he was an equipment manager, and a fucking horrible one at that, but we took him in as a young coach and tried to help him.

A friend of mine who would fly into town each game to help me in the booth really took this coach under his wing and financially assisted him throughout the entire 2018 season. I also let this guy borrow my car, borrow money, and tried to help him as much as possible, but, like my father always told me, "Don't trust anyone," and sure as shit, this guy tried to fuck me as well. This guy is the true definition of a slap dick coach, but he would end up being a fuck stick and a shit bird, which is why I fired him. He was highly incompetent and unable to perform the job description that was given to him. I guess he was sour about his dismissal from our program and tried firing shots at me on social media like the fucking coward little bitch he is. I would bet my beach house that this guy will never coach again. Nobody will ever hire him. If someone in this profession does hire this slap dick, I will give up coaching football altogether, but of course after I tell the slap dick who hired him all about himself.

This all happened within a few weeks of each other, just more of a reason that I needed to leave Indy. The text message would end up going viral and eventually make the board members cringe and fold up like a cheap lawn chair, which is probably why Indy had never been successful prior to my arrival. I was hoping the board and Dr. Barwick had a few more nuts and guts to stand up for me, but apparently they didn't want to fight for me, a person who had done quite a lot for a place that had nothing and built something very special in a short amount of time. This is the reason why you never trust anyone and always do what you feel is best.

I was the victim of a witch hunt, and I believe I was a scapegoat for something bigger that is coming down the pipe at Indy, but I won't be there to find out what that is. I was hurt and saddened by the lack of support from the powers that be, but it also wasn't surprising. At the end of the day, I know what I did for those kids and that community and how we put Indy on the college football map!

I will forever be grateful for my time at Indy, and I will never regret what I did, but I will learn, move on with my life, and await my next position, which will be to help others as I always have. I hopefully will build another program into an instant winner, which will always be what I strive for in life. I have had great success during my coaching career, and I know in my heart that I am far from done coaching kids and teaching others how to be great! I have been on top of mountains, just as I have been dragged through the mud, but one thing I do not know how to do is quit!

Jason Brown

Bonus Chapter

STOGIES

Cigars were introduced to me by James Fuller and Noah Drucker. James was my head coach in the Arena Football League, and Noah Drucker was a teammate of mine. The year was 2002, and we were over in Hawaii about to play the Hawaiian Islanders of the Arena Football League. We arrived on the island about four days prior to the game, so Coach Fuller

Jason Brown

allowed us to hang out at night and do some sightseeing. Noah had some cigars and offered me one, so I said sure, why not! The rest is history. I have become an avid cigar smoker and will always enjoy a good cigar along with some good whisky or cognac.

After *Last Chance U* (Indy) aired, the world saw me smoke cigars in my hot tub and have seen me smoke cigars in my Cadillacs. Due to that, I have received boatloads of cigars from different companies, as well as fans in general, which I am very appreciate of. I received some very good cigars and still have some left over from the season. I hope after this season I can get a new hot tub from a hot tub company! I smoke cigars just about anywhere: in my car, on the beach, at the house. Cigars, my dog Stogie, and being on a football field are my sanctuary. Those three things allow me to think freely and help me come up with my next plan of attack in life.

I have smoked just about every cigar made by just about every cigar manufacturer known to man. I have my favorites, and of course I love the Cubans, which I won't go into detail about in this book, but let me tell you, they are wonderful smokes. I like a strong maduro leaf with a 60-64 ring gauge (for my fans who feel compelled to send me a stick or two). Cigars

allow me to relax and escape the realities of the real world, even if it's for an hour or two. Many people ask me what allows me to escape and get away from everything? I respond by saying, "I am at peace when I smoke a stick, bust some spades, sip on some Maker's Mark and Coke, and being around my real friends and family."

When I first started coaching, I was introduced to dipping tobacco by a good friend of mine, Dave Portz, who is one of the best football coaches I have ever known. I went cold turkey after the first season at Indy. I was told I couldn't go cold turkey, and I said people who can't go cold turkey with an addiction are weak-minded fucks. Therefore, I dropped dipping Copenhagen that day! Smoking cigars and driving Cadillacs on the other hand, well, those are leisurely addictions that I won't be giving up.

STOGIE

I bought Stogie in December 2017 right after the season. He was six weeks old. Stogie has some strong genes and comes from a fifth-generation bloodline of pit bulls. He's mixed with Razors Edge and Genghis Khan. Stogie is now sixteen months old and quite a handful, but as loving a dog that you will ever find. And if you know anything about pits, you know they are as loyal as any dog in the world.

Stogie and I have quite the relationship; it's one of a football coach who has limited time and a dog who yearns for attention. I would bring Stogie into the office as a puppy during the winter months of 2018. Stogie quickly became part of the Indy family. He would bug the shit out of the coaches, and he quickly became the mascot on the practice field. The players loved him

and quickly adopted him as part of the team. He later would lead the team out of the tunnel at a home game.

Stogie was on the show with me as a puppy and quickly became a household name. I was bombarded with requests to start up his own social media account and create a Twitter page for him. I couldn't find the time to get that done, but I'm sure he would have had quite the following.

Stogie loves people; however, he is not too fond of other dogs, so I'm trying to break him in and teach him how to be nice and sweet like his owner! Stogie is very protective of me and suffers from separation anxiety, as many dogs who have been raised around their owner 24-7 often do. We frequently wrestle and have disputes, but he is family and will be a football dog for life! So, if you smoke cigars, please enjoy one for me, and if you love dogs, go love one for us, and stay tuned for the next chapter of our lives.

JB AND STOGIE OUT!
STAY TUNED FOR BIGGER & BETTER THINGS!

Review Requested:
If you loved this book, would you please provide a
review at Amazon.com?

CPSIA information can be obtained
at www.ICGtesting.com
Printed in the USA
LVHW110020300719
625827LV00004B/16/P